Civil War Experiences
With the New York Cavalry

Yours Truly
Henry C. Meyer

HENRY C. MEYER

Civil War Experiences With the New York Cavalry

Under Bayard, Gregg, Kilpatrick, Custer,
Raulston & Newberry 1862-1864

Henry C. Meyer

LEONAUR

Civil War Experiences
With the New York Cavalry
Under Bayard, Gregg, Kilpatrick, Custer,
Raulston & Newberry 1862-1864
by Henry C. Meyer

First published under the title
Civil War Experiences

Leonaur is an imprint
of Oakpast Ltd

ISBN: 978-0-85706-324-3 (hardcover)
ISBN: 978-0-85706-323-6 (softcover)

http://www.leonaur.com

Publisher's Notes

Contents

.

Introduction

During December, 1895, I received a letter from General Walter C. Newberry, of Chicago, who during the Civil War commanded the 24th New York Cavalry. In this the general wrote:

My Dear Major Meyer:

You will remember how urgent the boys were last summer for a history of the Regiment to be prepared. I resolved then to gratify them and am engaged on it now. I want you to aid me to the extent of giving me a detailed account of yourself—nativity, date of birth, former service, engagements that you were in that led up to your promotion, your service with us, your wounding and incidents accompanying it, your period of treatment in the Hospital, your civil record since, and be kind enough not to be at all modest in setting it all forth. I shall not use your language, neither shall I give you credit for the biography, and you may drop all modesty with me and give it to me in full. You may have kept something of a diary or there may be some old letters that you have written which will give me some record by dates of the Regiment's service. I want it all.

In 1896 I complied with this request to the extent of giving a brief account of my service in the army. Since then, members of my family and a few personal friends have asked me to incorporate in this account incidents that I recalled, some of which they had heard me relate, asserting that they would be of interest to my grandchildren.

The following story is my attempt to accede to these requests. I am naturally proud of having had the privilege of serving under the generals I have mentioned, and the story recited in the following pages is in accordance with my recollection of events that occurred over forty-five years ago.

New York, May, 1911.   Henry C. Meyer

CHAPTER 1

Enlistment

On the day Fort Sumter surrendered I was seventeen years old, having been born April 14, 1844. Like other boys, I proposed enlisting, but my father refused consent; and at that time youths under eighteen years would not be accepted without the consent of parents. In July of the following year, when the news of McClellan's retreat on the Peninsula was published, I was satisfied that the Government would need more men, and having carefully considered the matter, and being then eighteen years of age, I decided to go without my father's consent. Seeing a newspaper item to the effect that Captain Mallory, of the Harris Light Cavalry, had arrived in New York, and proposed to enlist some men for that regiment, I called upon him at the Metropolitan Hotel and made known my desire. He informed me that his recruiting office was not then arranged, though he had engaged a room a little farther up Broadway, and his sergeant was preparing to open it.

He seemed reluctant to take me, and talked to me as though I were too young to go, and as if I did not realize what I was about to undertake. I assured him that I had considered the matter well, and that I was physically strong; and that if he would not accept me I would try to enlist in Duryea's *Zouaves*, who were, at that time, enlisting men. He then told me to go up and see his sergeant and that he would come up later. I found the room, but the sergeant, however, had not yet unpacked the papers. On getting them opened he said he was unable to make them out, whereupon I asked him to let me examine them, and proceeded to make out my own enlistment papers, the sergeant watching me.

While I was thus engaged, a man with his arm off came in. He had just that day been discharged from the hospital, and inquired what steps he should take to get a pension, having been attracted by the flag hanging out of the office window. I noticed the sergeant was particularly anxious to get him out of the room, evidently not considering him a desirable acquisition to facilitate recruiting. I explained to the man what he should do. The sergeant, when he saw me make out my enlistment papers, remarked, "They won't keep you long in the ranks, because they can get better work for you to do," or words to that effect. I did not then comprehend what he meant, but my subsequent experience explained it. I was then sent to the examining physician, examined, passed, and sworn in for three years' service.

That night I went to my home, at Dobb's Ferry, on the Hudson River, and reported what I had done, intending to leave for Washington the next morning, when I was promised transportation. This interview with my parents was quite unpleasant, as my father was very angry and my mother in great distress. At that time both my father and his friends regarded my action as worse than foolish and almost as bad as though I had done something disreputable. Indeed, as I was afterwards informed, one gentleman remarked, "Well, that is too bad; that boy has gone to the devil, too."

The following morning I bade my parents goodbye, feeling that if I were wounded or crippled I should not care to return home for them to take care of me. Subsequent letters from home, however, removed that feeling. The following night, having received transportation, I sailed as the only passenger on a freight transport from a pier near the Battery to South Amboy. I well remember my feelings as I watched New York receding in the distance, there being no excitement or hand-shaking or waving of flags such as accompanied the departure of the first troops that left New York for thirty days' service the year before. From Amboy I went on a coal train to Philadelphia.

On landing at Walnut Street wharf I went into the soldiers' refreshment room, maintained by the citizens of Philadelphia, which was open night and day, and at which all soldiers passing through the city were fed free of charge. It was about two o'clock in the morning, very hot, and I was tired and depressed. Hence, when invited to partake of some refreshments, I was unable to do so but contented myself with eating a few pickles.

I then walked across the city to the Baltimore depot, which was then at the corner of Broad and Pine Streets, and took a passenger train for Baltimore, which I reached about seven o'clock in the morning, sitting up, as there were no sleeping-cars in those days. On arriving in Baltimore I walked to another part of the city to take the train for Washington. Meanwhile I wanted some breakfast. Going into a place which I supposed was a restaurant, I found that the only thing they could offer me was ice-cream. I thereupon ate some, and soon after took the train for Washington. In a few moments the Philadelphia pickles, the hot night, and the Baltimore ice-cream produced most severe cramps, and I was in a very distressed state of mind, fearing that I would never be able to reach the front, but would have to submit to the mortification of being returned home.

Arriving in Washington, I went to Willard's Hotel, and, after a good sleep, was able to take my dinner that evening. I had on citizen's clothes and was not recognized as a private soldier in the United States Army, so the head-waiter assigned me to a seat at a table where General Halleck, the commander-in-chief of the army, sat opposite.

That evening, my uncle, E.V. Price, who was in Washington, met me at the hotel and took me to General Pope's room. The latter had just arrived in Washington to take command of the Army of the Potomac. My uncle procured a pass from him to enable me to go through the lines and join my regiment, the Second New York Cavalry (Harris Light). It was stationed at Falmouth, Virginia. J. Mansfield Davies was the colonel at that time, and Judson Kilpatrick the lieutenant-colonel. My uncle, who knew Colonel Davies, introduced me to him that evening at the hotel. The following morning I accompanied him on the boat to Aquia Creek and reached the regiment on the evening of that day.

In two or three days I received my uniform and a horse was given to me. The fact that I had been seen coming into camp with the Colonel led some of the non-commissioned officers and men of my company to assume that I did not intend to serve in the ranks, but would likely be commissioned shortly and probably be jumped over them, who had already been out some time, though they had not been in any battle, their previous service being confined to drilling and a skirmish or two. This made it very unpleasant for me, and for a short time I was subjected to some little annoyance.

As I wore to the front the best suit of citizen's clothes I had, a man in our company by the name of Rufus West proposed to buy them and agreed to pay me eleven dollars for them. That night he deserted and joined Mosby's command, having made the remark before leaving that he did not "propose to fight to free niggers." He owes me the eleven dollars yet.

In a day or two I was assigned to picket duty with a man of my company, on the Rappahannock River, with instructions to keep a sharp lookout, as they said a female spy was expected to cross at that point. My comrade was Henry E. Johns, who enlisted from Hartford, Connecticut. He appeared to take pity on me, and that evening we discussed our families and our affairs; and at that time a warm attachment was formed, which lasted throughout the war, and since.

As we were to remain on guard all night, he suggested that we should take turns, each being on watch, two hours on, and two hours off. Before morning I found it extremely difficult to keep my eyes open, and several times walked to the river and washed my face in order to do so. Just before daylight it was my turn to go to sleep; when I awoke and looked around, I found no one on watch. Looking beside me I found my comrade, also asleep. The place at which we were posted was inaccessible in the night from our lines, because it was at the foot of a deep ravine. I don't imagine any female spy crossed at that point. If we had been caught asleep, however, it would have been an embarrassing position for both of us to have been placed in.

A few days later the Harris Light Cavalry made a raid in the neighborhood of Fredericks Hall, Virginia, in which movement the command marched some ninety miles in thirty hours. This was hard on the men, and many of them were confined to their tents on their return to camp, from saddle boils and lameness, for a day or two. I found it difficult to keep awake on the march and picket, yet I was able to do duty without interruption.

On this raid the regiment destroyed considerable property, and many of the men carried away all sorts of things for which they had no use. Indeed, I heard Colonel Kilpatrick laughingly remark that one fellow, in his zeal to have something, actually had a grindstone on his saddle in front of him. After carrying it about a mile he concluded, however, that he had no further use for it, and dropped it in the road

CORPORAL HENRY E. JOHNS

CHAPTER 2

Retreat from Rapidan

A few days afterwards the regiment marched through Culpeper and reached the battlefield of Cedar Mountain late on the day on which that engagement was fought. We approached the battlefield through what would be called the rear, where we first saw the horrible sights accompanying a battle, which are always dead horses, broken caissons, bodies lying on the ground, and the wounded. On the front line these sights are not so prominent.

The regiment was pushed to the front and placed on picket duty, I being posted on the edge of a piece of woods overlooking a valley, on the opposite side of which was Slaughter Mountain, where Stonewall Jackson's army was supposed to be.

While at my post on picket that night, an incident occurred which made a deep impression upon me, doubtless due to the time and place and the incidents of the preceding two weeks. Before leaving home, I had promised my mother that I would read at least one verse in my Testament each day. Not having done so that day was due to the fact that we had been marching and to the excitement attending the reaching of the battlefield and being put in position. I then took out my pocket Testament and went to a picket fire near where I was, leaning over to read a verse or two by its light, when I heard a rustle in the bushes. Immediately I grasped my weapons and was on the alert, when a coloured man crawled through the bushes and said to me, "What's that you got there, a Testament?" On admitting it, he said, "Do you know the chapter General Washington always used to read before he went into a fight?"

I told him I did not, whereupon he said, "You turn to the Ninety-first Psalm."

"Now," he said, "you read it." I then read aloud:

Surely He shall deliver thee from the snare of the fowler and from the noisome pestilence.

He shall cover thee with His feathers and under His wings shalt thou trust; His truth shall be thy shield and buckler.

Thou shalt not be afraid for the terror by night nor for the arrow that flieth by day.

Nor for the pestilence that walketh in darkness, nor for the destruction that wasteth at noon day.

A thousand shall fall at thy side and ten thousand at thy right hand; but it shall not come nigh thee.

At the reading of each of these verses he exclaimed, "You see, he didn't get hit." The contraband evidently was perfectly sincere in the belief that if I read this verse before a battle I would never get hurt. He then went away. This incident, coupled with the facts that I had only been about ten days away from home, that I had seen the horrible sights of the battlefield the previous afternoon, that I could see the enemy's camp-fires across the valley, and that I was wondering what fate was in store for me the following day,—all tended to impress this incident upon my mind.

The next morning the regiment advanced to the Rapidan River, presumably with the object of searching for the flank of Jackson's army. Just above the ford, which I think was Robertson's, was the residence of the Confederate General Taliaferro. Our picket line was between the house and the river. Captain Walters of my regiment had arranged with Mrs. Taliaferro to have breakfast at her house. She and her niece were engaged in a good-natured altercation with some of the men of my company, she repeatedly remarking, "I want you men to understand that I am the granddaughter of Chief-Justice Marshall of the United States."

When she had said this several times an Irishman of my company remarked, "And who the divil is he anyhow?" The disgust on her face may well be imagined.

I had been polite in my remarks to her when she turned upon me and asked, "Aren't you from New Orleans?"

I told her, "No," that I was from New York, when she shook her head sadly and said, "Well, I'm surprised that apparently such a nice young man as you should be engaged in such a wicked cause as this."

The laughter of my comrades which greeted this remark was followed by their teasing me the rest of the campaign, calling me, "The nice young man and the wicked cause."

About this time the pickets began firing, when Captain Walters remarked, "I will go down and see what the matter is." He mounted his horse, started down the hill toward the ford, and in a moment or two was brought back dead, their sharpshooters having shot him through the heart immediately after he left the house. This was the first time I had heard bullets whistle.

That night Stonewall Jackson's movement to the flank and rear of Pope's army resulted in the recall of the cavalry and a night march through Culpeper to Brandy Station. We bivouacked for the night, but did not unsaddle. About daybreak we were attacked. Although I heard bullets whistle at the Rapidan River, where Captain Walters was killed, this was the first real engagement I was in. In the early part of it we were supporting the skirmish line.

Later in the day the battalion in which my company was made a charge, led by Major Henry E. Davies, in which a number were killed and wounded, and some confusion ensued by reason of a railroad cut, into which the command rode, its existence not being known when the charge was ordered. Prior to this, in the retreating movements of that morning, my horse, which had become blind from the hard marching of the night before, fell in a ditch with me. He struggled out, and I was able to remount him, though we were quite hard pressed by the advancing enemy.

The Harris Light Cavalry was one of the regiments of General George D. Bayard's brigade, which for sixteen successive days was under fire and engaged in most arduous service in covering the retreat of Pope's army and watching the fords on the Rappahannock River to detect the crossing of General Lee's troops. This continuous service terminated with the second battle of Bull Run, where Lieutenant Compton, the only remaining officer with my company, was killed. This occurred the evening before the last day of the battle.

CHAPTER 3

Second Battle at Bull Run

There had been some very severe fighting on the part of King's division. We approached the field from Manassas Junction, arriving about nine o'clock. As we were riding through this division, the men called out, "What regiment is that?" When we told them they arose and cheered us, for we had been with them on a former occasion.

Then, as we were approaching the Centerville pike, Kilpatrick rode down the column calling out, "General MacDowell wants the Harris Light to take a battery." "Draw sabres." We drew sabres, put our cap bands under our chins, and turned into the pike, then to the left, moving a short distance, and then into a field, also on the left, forming in column of squadrons. It was then too dark to see any distance ahead. My position was within one or two of the flank of my company, where I heard Kilpatrick order my squadron to go out into the road to charge this battery, which we could not see.

As we were not the last squadron in the column, which happened to be Captain Seymour's, he said, "Never mind, take the last one," which was fortunate for us. In a moment or two we heard the clatter of the horses' hoofs on the pike, and then saw a sheet of fire from the enemy's lines some distance ahead, which I understood was on the edge of a piece of woods. This fire was also doing damage to our columns exposed to it, when the order was given for us to "wheel and retire," where we could get under cover.

From this unfortunate charge only eleven men came back that night. It was said that they were subjected to not only the fire of the enemy but also from our infantry on the right of the road, who, hearing the clatter of the horses' hoofs, and unable to see what caused it, assumed it to be a charge of the enemy's cavalry, when they also opened fire. It was felt at the time that the ordering of this charge was a blunder, and yet it was one of the many blunders from which our volunteer army constantly suffered in the early years of the war. Kilpatrick was severely criticised in the regiment for it that night and the next day; little, however, was ever said about it in the reports. Whether Kilpatrick acted under superior orders or on his own initiative, I never learned.

A few minutes after the regiment had retired a short distance, Sergeant Griswold came up and reported to Kilpatrick in my hearing that the enemy were advancing their lines, that our wounded were being captured, and that Lieutenant Compton of my company had been killed, and he showed where a bullet had passed through the collar of his coat as he wheeled when asked to surrender. Kilpatrick called for somebody to go with him as an orderly, as he wanted to find General Bayard and General McDowell. This I did, holding his horse while he was in conference with these generals that night.

The next morning we recovered the body of Lieutenant Compton, of whom we were very fond, and we succeeded in making a coffin out of three cracker-boxes from which we took out the ends; wrapping him in a blanket we buried him in this cracker-box coffin at the corner of the old stone house on the Centerville Pike. His friends subsequently recovered his remains. We all felt rather blue over the loss of comrades in the affair of the night before, which had seemed to us so needless.

Among the pathetic incidents of that morning was one which indicated the unselfish heroism of a young soldier. Early in the day some of our men were looking over the battlefield of the night before for missing comrades, and one, I remember, spoke of having found a young boy, apparently not over eighteen years of age, lying with his shattered leg in a pool of blood. My comrade spoke to him saying, "I will go and get somebody to help carry you off," whereupon, the wounded boy faintly remarked: "I do not think you can do me any good, but during the night I heard groans coming from over the hill yonder, and I think if you go there you may be able to save some one; but if you will give me a drink of water I will be much obliged."

The man gave his canteen to the wounded boy and started off for help. On his return he found the boy, with the canteen clasped in his hands, dead.

During the morning the armies were getting in position for the final struggle of the afternoon of that day, which, I think, was the thirty-first of August. Our regiment was lying in column of fours awaiting orders. That afternoon, with a view to saving our horses from the effect of shells dropping near us, Kilpatrick got permission to move the column to the right a little, so as to be out of range. While we were making this movement he happened to be riding alongside of me, I being in the ranks, when a staff-officer approached and greeted him, evidently some friend that he had known at West Point or in the regular army.

This officer leaned forward and said in an earnest manner, "Whose cavalry is this?"

Kilpatrick told him it was his. I then heard him say, "General Porter," meaning Fitz-John Porter, "is fearful that there is going to be a break. I wish you would deploy your cavalry in the rear of our lines and do not allow a man to pass through unless he is wounded."

Whereupon Kilpatrick gave the order "By fours, left about wheel," and moved the regiment left in front and then into line, with the men at intervals in close skirmishing order. We no sooner had gotten into line and advanced toward the woods in which Fitz-John Porter's corps was, on the left of our army, than I heard the most terrific crashes of artillery and then the rattle of musketry. This was Longstreet's corps opening on us. In a few moments Porter's men came swarming out of the woods.

After them came the Confederates, with their batteries close up with their infantry. Several times I saw our regiments rally, but they were completely overpowered and swept away, resistance being apparently impossible. It was this attack of Longstreet's with a superior force which Porter had predicted and which General Pope had refused to believe possible, which resulted in the crushing of the left of our army, and the defeat of General Pope at the second battle of Bull Run.

Having overheard the anxious message of General Porter's staff-officer to Colonel Kilpatrick, I assumed that it was my duty to carry out instructions literally, that is, I tried to stop every man I could from passing to the rear. When all our guns at that part of the field had limbered up, except those of one regular battery, I met a squad of men with a major making for the rear. I rode up and told them to go and lie down beside this battery until I could get more men to act as a support. He demurred, stating that it was no use, and at my remonstrating with him, one of his men, an Irishman, spoke up and said, "Who the divil are you to be talking that way to our officer?"

However, the major and his squad went with me and lay down alongside the battery, when I started for another squad. I had gone but

Major General Judson Kilpatrick

a few rods when the major got up and went over the hill with his men. In the light of what I learned afterwards, the major and those who had seen fighting on the Peninsula had a better idea of the proper thing to do than I did with my boyish inexperience; for that was no place for them to remain at that time.

I then discovered that my regiment had withdrawn. When I rode up to the commander of this battery, as he was limbering up his guns to retire, the enemy being almost up to him, and told him that I had been instructed to keep back stragglers, and asked him what I had better do, he smiled and replied, "The best thing you can do is to get out of here." I then proposed to stay with him until I found General Bayard.

Pretty soon I met General Pope with his staff, and subsequently General Bayard, who commanded our brigade. Riding up to the latter I asked him if he knew where my regiment was. He turned and inquired where certain members of his staff and orderlies were, and on being told that some had had their horses shot, and reasons being given for the absence of others, he said, "You stay with me."

I then rode with him over to the right, to the railroad cut, where Sigel's men had been fighting. I well recall how angry General Bayard was, talking to himself and shaking his fist, evidently in a rage at the bad management which had resulted in the defeat of our army. About ten o'clock that night Major Henry E. Davies of my regiment reported to General Bayard where the regiment was, and asked for instructions. It was back somewhere on the Centerville pike. I then asked the General if I might go back with Major Davies, as my little gray horse had only one shoe on, to which he consented.

The next day the regiment marched to Alexandria and reached the hills behind that town at night during a terrific rainstorm. I succeeded in getting into a barn, where I slept soundly in my wet clothes until the sun was up the following morning. I well remember the sensation when I awoke and saw the dome of the Capitol at Washington in the distance.

Going into the town I got weighed in front of a sutler's tent, and, to my surprise, I had gained five pounds since I had enlisted six weeks before.

CHAPTER 4

Advance After Antietam

At this time the regiment had one hundred and fifty-two men, as I recall it, present for duty; there were eleven men and no officers in my company. We were ordered to Ball's Cross Road to refit, where we got new clothing and horses; a number of recruits were sent to us, and some of our sick and wounded men returned to duty. We were then sent out in the neighborhood of Centerville, where we were engaged in scouting and skirmishing with the enemy's cavalry while the Army of the Potomac was in Maryland during the Antietam campaign.

On the return of Lee's army to Virginia, my regiment in Bayard's brigade was engaged in the various movements on the advance to Fredericksburg. The incident I most readily recall during this movement was the relieving of General McClellan from the command of the army and superseding him by General Burnside. At that time the army idolized McClellan. I went to a stream for water one night, where I met an infantryman. He looked so badly that I asked him what the matter was, when he replied, "Haven't you heard the news?"

I said, "No."

He then told me that General McClellan had been removed, whereupon he began to cry. I went back to our bivouac, as we were on the march, and reported this. I recall that we sat up in groups till well into the night discussing this, and our conclusion was that we were being used as an examining board to try candidates for the next presidency.

Of course, in writing of our impressions from our limited point of view at that time, I do not wish to convey the idea that I now think McClellan should not have been superseded. The only mistake was in selecting the man that superseded him.

In due time the captain of my company, J. F. B. Mitchell, finding out that I had some clerical ability, as the sergeant who was present when I made out my enlistment papers prophesied, detailed me to make out the company's pay-rolls and do whatever company writing there was to do, in consideration of which I was, for the time being, relieved from doing guard duty. This fact was known to the members of my company who were then very friendly to me.

The night before the battle of Fredericksburg I was on picket on the river's bank opposite the town, where I heard the enemy's artillery being put in position and men making speeches to the troops. During the battle, the regiment was on the field in reserve, occasionally under fire from shells but otherwise not actively engaged. General Bayard, our brigade commander, was mortally wounded by a shell, dying the next day, the date set for his wedding, he having requested a postponement of his leave of absence when he learned there was to be a battle. When our regiment recrossed the Rappahannock I had no idea the army had been defeated; indeed, until we saw the New York papers we were ignorant of the fact.

Chapter 5

The Stoneman Raid

Shortly after the battle of Fredericksburg, Captain Henry C. Weir, the adjutant-general of the division to which General D. McM. Gregg had then been assigned, asked an orderly who happened to be a member of my company, and who was then engaged carrying a despatch to his headquarters, if he could suggest a man in his regiment whom he could detail to act as clerk to make out returns and reports, his former clerk having gone home with the body of General Bayard. The man suggested me, and was told to request me to report to division headquarters.

I remember being quite startled at this order, and, anxious to look as presentable as possible, I stripped and bathed in a brook, on the edges of which the ice had formed, before calling on Captain Weir. He questioned me as to my occupation before entering the army, which had been that of a clerk in my uncle's firm, T. B. Coddington & Co., metal importers, whom he knew by reputation. He also stated that he knew of my father's home on the Hudson River. Indeed, he manifested an interest in me, and, after giving me a copy of a tri-monthly report to look at, asked me if I thought I could consolidate the several regimental reports, copies of which he showed me.

I made the attempt and succeeded, whereupon he said he would ask General Gregg to have me detailed at his headquarters. That detail was made out in December, 1862. Though my rank was still that of a private, my position was much improved and my surroundings much more pleasant. I was treated with great consideration by Captain Weir, and was thereafter busily engaged while in winter quarters in performing the duties of an adjutant-general's clerk, which included such writing as General Gregg required of me.

At the time of the battle of Chancellorsville, Gregg's division went

Brevet Lieutenant Colonel H. C. Weir

on what was known as the Stoneman raid to Richmond. On this movement and subsequently on the march, and in all engagements as long as I was with the general, I was sent with messages and orders the same as a staff-officer.

On this raid I attracted the attention of General Gregg and the headquarters staff by my ability to sleep on horseback when on the march. Captain Weir had given me a fine horse, which happened to be a very fast walker. It was General Gregg's custom to ride alone at the head of his staff, occasionally inviting Dr. Phillips, the medical director of the division, to ride alongside of him. As soon as I would fall asleep, the bridle reins would naturally slacken and the horse begin to forge ahead. My position in the column was in rear of the officers of the staff, and with the general's orderly and bugler.

Instead of restraining the horse, my comrades and the staff officers would open the way and urge him along while I, sitting upright but fast asleep, would ride alongside of our dignified general and sometimes ahead of him before he noticed me, when invariably he would wake me up, grabbing me by the arm and saying, "Meyer, wake up."

Chagrined I would return to my place, the staff officers and orderlies greatly amused. This incident occurred so frequently on this Stoneman raid that it evidently made an impression on the general, because, meeting him some twenty years after the war at a reunion in Philadelphia he, on greeting me, introduced me to a group of officers and immediately recalled the fact of my so often being asleep on horseback.

One day my horse strayed from the road and followed a fence up a bank until he came to a point where the slope reached the fence and he could go no farther, when the general called out, "Wake him up, he will break his neck." The jolt of the horse, however, sliding down the slope into the road awakened me, though I did not fall off. The only penalty I suffered from sleeping on horseback was the occasional loss of a cap and the scratching of my face by the branches of trees, but it undoubtedly had much to do with my being able to withstand the fatigue incident to our campaigns, since the fact is that I never was off duty for a single hour, by reason of sickness, during my whole term of service.

CHAPTER 6

Battle at Brandy Station

On the 9th of June, 1863, occurred the battle of Brandy Station, in which more cavalry were engaged than in any battle of the Civil War. General Buford's division had crossed the Rappahannock River at Beverly Ford early in the morning. General Gregg's division crossed at Kelly's Ford, and General Duffie farther down the river, the latter being under General Gregg's command and supposed to accompany him. As we were approaching Brandy Station we heard the heavy cannonading of Buford's attack, when General Gregg, with the brigades of Colonel Windham and Colonel Kilpatrick, hurried to the battlefield. Around the station and between Culpeper and the Rappahannock the country was open and favourable for cavalry engagements. Indeed, there was one there at every advance and retreat of the army during 1862 and 1863, I being present at three of them.

As soon as we emerged from the woods near the station we saw the enemy on a hill near the Barber House, which was General Stuart's headquarters. We were approaching them practically in their rear; their artillery, however, firing at us. General Gregg at once ordered Colonel Windham to charge with his three regiments—the First New Jersey, the First Pennsylvania, and the First Maryland; Kilpatrick's brigade at the time was coming on the field to our right. Windham charged this hill in columns of regiments, and it was a very thrilling sight to see these troops going up the slope in the bright June sun, their sabres glistening.

As they neared the enemy General Gregg showed an enthusiasm that I had never noticed before. He started his horse on a gallop toward the house, swinging his gauntlets over his head and hurrahing, at the same time telling Captain Weir to ride over and direct Kilpatrick to charge at once. Captain Weir happened to be riding a horse that would always refuse a fence unless another went first. At this critical moment his horse shied twice, when mine took the fence and I started to carry the order.

As soon as my horse went over Captain Weir's immediately followed. As he was the adjutant-general and directed to take the order, I rode up the hill supposing that when Kilpatrick's brigade got there the enemy would be routed and I might get a prisoner. On arriving at Stuart's headquarters I found Windham's brigade in a hand-to-hand fight around the house. Here I met a flanking party of the enemy, who were driving back a portion of General Windham's command, Kilpatrick's men not then having reached that point.

In the fight about these headquarters I saw a Confederate officer sabre a man who I believe belonged to the Maryland regiment; and although the man begged for quarter, I saw this officer strike him twice after he offered to surrender. I tried to shoot him, but the ball from my pistol missed him and struck his horse. This did not take immediate effect. Finding that I was about to be cut off, as Windham's command had been repulsed and Kilpatrick had not arrived, and having only one charge left in my revolver, I had to allow the officer to ride up to strike me, so as to be sure of my aim.

As I presented the pistol, it missed fire, and as soon as he could recover his seat in the saddle he struck at me. I had, however, fallen down on the neck of my horse, so the point of the sabre cut into my collar-bone, but the weight of the blow cut a two-quart pail, that I had borrowed that morning to cook coffee in, nearly in two. Before either of us could recover control of our horses, I had gotten my sabre in my hand, which had been hanging by a knot from my wrist, as was the custom. He then struck at me the second time, which blow I parried. His horse then sank under him. I was then being crowded in a corner, where a fence joined a building, by four of his followers, one of whom was dismounted.

The latter I saw shooting at me. Urging my horse he jumped a fence and then a ditch beyond it. This enabled me to escape with only the loss of my hat. I was particularly anxious not to be captured, because before going into the action the general had confided to me, for safe-keeping, all his despatches and instructions, which it was my custom to carry about my person, as, wearing a private's uniform, in the event of capture, there would be less liability of my being searched than in the case of a staff-officer wearing the uniform of an adjutant-general.

I finally joined some of our men near the railroad station, but could not find the general; so, for the time being, I reported to an officer of the First New Jersey cavalry, whom I knew, and remained with him until we were again cut off by a force of the enemy. Later in the day I found General Gregg, who, I was told, had been quite anxious lest I had been captured, for someone had reported that he had seen me hard pressed by the enemy, and he supposed I was captured, and the general knew I had his papers in my pocket.

My wound was not dangerous, though painful, and that night, after it was plastered up by the doctor, I sat up and made out a list of the casualties of the division during the day. When it was suggested by Adjutant-General Weir, that I include my name, I remarked that I thought I would not do it, as seeing it in the newspapers would needlessly alarm my mother, and that it did not amount to anything serious, and wasn't worthwhile. After the war, however, on the advice of friends, I reported this circumstance to the War Department and had it certified by both General Gregg and Colonel Weir,[1] who are still living, merely to make it a part of my record there on file.

Kilpatrick's men soon reached the house, capturing Stuart's adjutant-general and his papers. The fighting was desperate; charges being made, repulsed, and repeated by our men against a much larger force, as Duffie's brigade had failed to report. Finally, the Confederates bringing infantry from Culpeper, our commands were withdrawn, without molestation by the enemy, across the Rappahannock, the purpose of the movement being accomplished; which was to cripple Stuart's cavalry, to prevent his starting on a raid to Pennsylvania which was contemplated, and also to ascertain if Lee's army was still in that vicinity. It was also a great benefit to our troops engaged, in giving them experience in fighting in large bodies mounted, with sabres, and added much to their confidence, as was demonstrated in later engagements.

After the battle, meeting the man who loaned me his tin pail which had been destroyed by the sabre blow I described, I explained to him how it happened, when, to my surprise, he complainingly remarked, "Well, how do you suppose I am going to cook my coffee?" Whereupon, I remarked, "Well, I can't help it, but I will give you a new pail as soon as I can buy one." Evidently the loss of his coffee boiler was of more consequence to him than my narrow escape.

1. See Appendix B.

CHAPTER 7

Battles at Aldie, Middleburgh and Upperville

In about ten days General Gregg's division marched towards Aldie, the object being to discover the movements of Lee's army; the idea being that our cavalry should find their cavalry, attack and drive them back on their infantry, thus obtaining the knowledge the commander of the army required. On this march to Aldie General Pleasanton, the corps commander, was represented at General Gregg's headquarters by one of his staff officers, Captain George A. Custer, afterwards General. When Custer appeared he at once attracted the attention of the entire command. (*My Life on the Plains or Personal Experiences With Indians* by George A. Custer also published by Leonaur.)

On that day he was dressed like an ordinary enlisted man, his trousers tucked in a pair of short-legged government boots, his horse equipments being those of an ordinary wagonmaster. He rode with a little rawhide riding whip stuck in his bootleg, and had long yellow curls down to his shoulders, his face ruddy and good-natured.

While on this march we came to a stream beside the road, in which a full battalion could water their horses at once. As the headquarters staff and the troops following us had gone into line to permit their horses to drink, Custer, for some reason, concluded to go in on the other side of the stream, riding in alone to allow his horse to drink. He did not know how deep the water was, and after his horse was satisfied, instead of returning by the way he went in, concluded to cross the stream and come out on our side. The water was deeper than he anticipated and his horse nearly lost his footing.

However, when he got to our side, he urged his horse to climb out at a point where the bank was steep. In this effort he fell over backward, Custer going out of sight in the water. In an instant, however, he was up on his feet and the horse struggled out amid the shouts of the spectators, when, mounting his horse, the march was resumed. The dust at this time was so thick that one could not see more than a set of fours ahead, and in a few minutes, when it settled on his wet clothes and long wet hair, Custer was an object that one can better imagine than I can describe.

In a short time, Kilpatrick, at the head of our column, met Fitzhugh Lee's command at Aldie, and drove it through the town, where a desperate fight occurred just beyond it, the enemy being strongly posted there behind stone walls. As soon as the first shots were heard, General Gregg hurried to the front and took his position on a hill just beyond and to the right of the town, upon which Kilpatrick had posted a battery. It was then found that Kilpatrick was outnumbered, all his command had been charging and he had no reserves.

General Gregg then directed me to go back and bring Colonel Irwin Gregg, commanding the Second Brigade, by a short cut back of the town, through the woods, to this part of the field as quickly as possible. Just as I went over the ridge to carry this order, I met the First Maine cavalry, with Colonel Doughty at its head, coming onto the field. As I passed him, the colonel, who knew me, laughingly remarked, "You are going in the wrong direction."

I replied: "Yes, I know it, but I will be back in a few minutes."

Very shortly I returned to this spot with Colonel Gregg at the head of his brigade, when I saw a man leading a horse upon which was a body, evidently dead, as his arms were hanging on one side and the feet on the other, a man supporting it. Inquiring, "Whom have you got there?" the man replied, "Colonel Doughty."

The colonel, who was a most gallant man, as soon as he arrived on the field at a moment most critical for Kilpatrick, charged at the head of his regiment, routing a charge of the enemy that had repulsed the Fourth New York, and then charged upon dismounted men behind stone walls, where he received two bullets through his breast. It was reported that night that some of the prisoners we had taken had said that the old fellow riding at the head of his regiment seemed so brave they hated to shoot him. This charge, however, routed the enemy, and, Irwin Gregg having arrived with his remaining regiments, they withdrew.

That night was rather a blue time for us. Lieutenant Whitaker, a fine officer of my regiment, was among the killed, and the First Mas-

Brevet Major General D. McM. Gregg

sachusetts cavalry had suffered severely. Our men induced a wheel-wright in the village to work that night making coffins for some of the officers who had been killed.

On the second day after occurred the fight at Middleburg. On this occasion Colonel Irwin Gregg's brigade had the advance. The enemy had been forced back to a strong position on a ridge, their lines occupying the right and left of the turnpike in the edge of woods covering the ridge on both sides of the road. On the right, in front of the enemy, was a cleared field, on the far side of which were also woods in which Colonel Gregg had two of his regiments, one dismounted, and one mounted ready to charge at a favourable moment. The Tenth New York cavalry was down the road in reserve.

The enemy's battery was posted on the left of the pike and on our right as we faced them. Just below this battery, the ground receding, was a large wheat field and behind a stone wall parallel to the pike they had a line of dismounted men, their battery firing into the woods where Colonel Gregg's two regiments were. General Gregg was with our battery on a ridge some distance back. As the enemy were making a determined stand General Gregg turned to me and said: "Ride up to Colonel Gregg, present my compliments, and ask him why he does not drive those people out of there."

As I rode to deliver this message I wondered how Colonel Gregg would receive it from me, who was not then a commissioned officer, though he knew me as the general's clerk.

When I reached the woods in which his command was, I started to ride in, when an orderly holding a couple of horses called out, "Here, you can't go mounted through there."

Asking him then if Colonel Gregg was in there he replied that he was, and that he was holding his horse. Leaving my horse with this man I walked through the woods on the edge of which was Colonel Gregg's line. He was standing with his shoulder against a tree at the very front of it. As I approached him he reached out, grabbed me by the arm, saying, "Keep back, they will hit you," and drew me up alongside of him where we were somewhat protected by the tree. He then said, "Well, what is it?"

I then repeated General Gregg's message, expecting an irritated reply, since it seemed to imply a censure. Instead of that, he, in the mildest manner possible, said: "I will tell you. You see their line across this clearing?" Replying "Yes," he continued: "You see where their guns are on the right of the road covering this, and you also see a line of dismounted men behind that stone wall at the wheat field. Now, if I order a charge across there it will be subjected to an enfilading fire from those men behind the wall and it will be very expensive of men."

He then asked me if the general had a spare regiment that he could send around in a ravine beyond the wheat field, have them dismount and crawl through the wheat unobserved and attack the men who were facing him from behind the stone wall. I told him there was, and he asked me to go back and explain the matter, saying, "If the General will send some men to get those fellows started behind that wall I will charge." I returned and described the situation to General Gregg, who directed a battalion of the Harris Light, I think, to make a detour, crawl through the wheat field, and attack the men behind the wall, who were practically right under the guns of the enemy, which were, however, firing over their heads across the road into the woods from which they were expecting a charge to be made.

The general then directed me to return and tell Colonel Gregg to charge as soon as the men behind the stone wall were attacked. In due time the Harris Light suddenly appeared only a few rods in the rear of the Confederates behind the wall, who, without any warning, received a volley in their backs. They were at once in confusion and at that moment the bugle sounded the charge and the First Maine and Fourth Pennsylvania from the woods, and the Tenth New York in column on the turnpike, charged and took the ridge, the Confederate battery getting away just in the nick of time.

I recall seeing the body of one of their colonels lying out in the turnpike just near where their guns had stood. This finished the fight for that day. This incident is mentioned somewhat in detail because I think that Colonel Gregg's coolness and solicitude for the safety of his men, where, by the use of a little strategy a needless loss of life was saved, deserve recognition.

The following day, which I think was Sunday, the three divisions of the cavalry corps, including General Gregg's, drove the enemy steadily back without much resistance on their part until we reached Upperville. There was open country at the outskirts of the town, and to the left as we approached it were woods. As our men attempted to charge down the main street they were met by a murderous fire from behind a high hedge, and at the same moment the enemy charged from the woods on the left and drove them back. For a few minutes the situation seemed most critical, and just then a piece of shell struck General

Gregg's horse in the stomach behind the saddle girth, grazing the general's leg. The horse sank under him and in an instant one of his orderlies dismounted, gave the general his horse, and took the saddle from the wounded animal.

At this moment General Gregg ordered a cavalry regiment, I think the Sixth Regulars, who were nearby in a field, to make a counter charge, which, after a little delay caused by the presence of a stone wall, they did. This charge, with our men, who rallied, co-operating, resulted in driving the enemy back into and through the town. To our surprise, the general's wounded horse had struggled to his feet and was running beside him with his nose against his leg, his entrails dragging on the ground. Noticing this, he exclaimed, "For God's sake, somebody shoot him!" Whereupon I discharged my pistol in the horse's ear, which killed him.

Just then, as we approached the entrance to the town, I heard Nick, the general's bugler, calling me to come and help him. Looking around I found Nick trying to ward off the blows of an infuriated German of our army, who was trying to sabre a Confederate boy who had been wounded and was lying down on his horse's neck. I immediately interfered, and with my sabre parried a blow intended for the boy, when the German excitedly exclaimed, "Vy, he's a Reb," when I replied, "Suppose he is, can't you see he's done for?" Whereupon, after a brief altercation the German rode on.

Nick then led the boy's horse out, and the command moved on, the enemy having broken. We soon met one of our doctors, and being anxious to know if the boy was mortally wounded, we took him to a nearby house where three ladies came to the gate, and, when they saw it was a Confederate soldier, began to cry. We carried him to a room, turned a chair up for him to recline on, when the doctor opened his shirt and found a bullet had entered his breast. The boy turned to the women who were standing around, pointed to little Nick, and faintly remarked, "There's the only friend I had today." We then left the doctor with him, mounted our horses, rode on, and soon joined the general.

The enemy were driven to Ashby's Gap. This battle and those of the preceding days demonstrated the fact that Lee's army was on its way to Maryland.

CHAPTER 8

March to Gettysburg

General Hooker, commander of the Army of the Potomac, having been satisfied, as a result of the cavalry engagements here described, that General Lee intended to invade Maryland, Gregg's division, as did the rest of the army in a few days, crossed the Potomac at Edward's Ferry at night. It was moonlight, and I, in common with others, experienced a strange sensation as we watched our columns crossing the pontoon bridges, the bands playing, *Maryland, my Maryland.* We then marched for Frederick, reaching that city before noon of the next day.

As we rode down its main street we witnessed a sight the like of which we had been unfamiliar with, since in Virginia, being the enemy's country, the people when we entered a town either concealed themselves, or, when seen, showed by their demeanor that they either detested or feared us. In Frederick, however, every house was decorated and the porches filled with people enthusiastically waving and making every demonstration of delight. We soon after marched through Liberty and to New Windsor. In the former place we met our infantry passing through the town as we rode in. Here we saw ladies with servants standing in the streets beside the marching column, handing out cakes, milk, and lemonade to the tired and dusty infantrymen, who were not permitted to halt, one lady remarking in my presence, "Isn't it a shame that they won't allow them to rest."

Later in the day we stopped at New Windsor, where the general made his headquarters at the little village hotel. Near this hotel, Johns, the general's orderly, and I were offered refreshments by a lady who kept a young ladies' boarding school. At this school were about fourteen enthusiastic young girls who overwhelmed us with attentions. Indeed, they took the ribbons from their necks and braided the manes of our horses with them, and mine had a red, white, and blue rosette attached to his forelock. We soon moved on, but that night the general was ordered to return to this town.

On getting this information I mentioned it to my comrade Johns, and suggested that as soon as it got a little dark we should ride on ahead of the column, when we might again meet the schoolgirls, which we subsequently did. The general made his headquarters at the little hotel beside the school-building, and we took our horses inside the village cemetery adjoining the school-grounds and tied them to the fence, taking off the saddles, and spreading our blankets on the ground. As we were drawing them over our heads on turning in for the night, we heard a call from one of the upper windows of the school, which was filled with faces, telling us to remember our dreams, for dreams dreamt on a strange pillow often came true.

We knew no more till about daylight, when we awakened and found it had been raining. While we were feeding and grooming our horses, a servant came to us with an invitation from the mistress of the school, stating that breakfast would be ready for us in a few minutes, and that we would find water, soap, and towels on the back porch where we "might refresh ourselves." We soon repaired to the porch where we found two white china basins, and fresh water, soap, and towels. This was a novelty, as hitherto a piece of a grain bag which we carried in our saddle-pocket was what we used when a towel was necessary. The breakfast-table was spread on the back porch.

Noticing the general's horse saddled, we expressed a fear that he might start while we were at breakfast, when the lady proposed to have the table removed to the front porch where we could see the general when he came out to mount. This was done and at this most bountiful meal we had about a dozen girls to wait on us, each with her album for us to write our autographs in. The general soon appeared, when, thanking the ladies for their hospitality, we moved on.

As soon as Captain Weir, the adjutant-general, saw me he began to censure me for being absent that night as he had a lot of writing to do which I should have done, when one of the staff-officers, noticing my horse's mane and the rosette on his forelock, pointed them out to him. He, evidently appreciating the situation, withheld any further comment.

Within the next day or so we marched to Westminster and to Manchester, leaving the latter place by daylight for York, where it was reported the Confederate cavalry were, and Gregg was sent to attack them. We reached the hills beyond York some time that afternoon and saw their pickets. Just at this time a despatch was received from the corps commander stating that fighting had begun at Gettysburg and that General Gregg was to report there with his command with all possible speed. He thereupon started the column for Gettysburg by way of Hanover.

We marched the rest of that afternoon and through the night, reaching Hanover about two o'clock in the morning. As in many Pennsylvania towns, this had a public square, at one end of which was a market-house with a road on either side of it, and the general had to awaken some of the citizens to ascertain which was the direct road to Gettysburg. We noticed dead horses in the streets of Hanover, and the citizens told us of the fight Kilpatrick's division had had there the afternoon before, in which he succeeded in driving away the Confederate cavalry that attacked him as he was passing through the town.

While the general was waiting to ascertain the right road to Gettysburg, I fell asleep sitting on a zinc-covered fish stall, my bridle rein in my hand. On awaking I discovered the command had all moved on; learning the road they took, I hurried on and soon overtook them.

CHAPTER 9

Repulse of Stuart

General Gregg reached the battlefield of Gettysburg about noon and reported to the commanding general, whose headquarters were not far from the cemetery, where I noticed that the sod and the graves were much torn up by artillery wheels. The general was ordered with his division to take position on the right of our army. During the day a portion of the command did some skirmishing, and our artillery occasionally fired when the enemy appeared, but we were not heavily engaged. This was the second of July, the day on which the fighting was so severe on the left of our line, where Longstreet's corps made such desperate attempts to break through in the vicinity of the Round Tops.

The weather was extremely hot and it was on this, the second day of the battle, that the Sixth Corps made a march of about thirty-two miles to reach the field, their exhausted and sun-struck men lying for fifteen miles on the road. The following, the third and last day of the battle, General Gregg's division was, at his suggestion, moved to a position farther to the right and rear, to guard against the enemy's breaking through to where our reserve artillery and ammunition were parked.

About noon a despatch was sent to him stating that General Howard reported that heavy clouds of dust were seen rising above the trees on his right, indicating that a large force of cavalry was moving in that direction. General Custer with his brigade, which belonged to General Kilpatrick's division but had been under General Gregg's orders, was about to return to Kilpatrick, who was on the left of the army, when General Gregg proposed to Custer that, in view of an attack from a strong force which now seemed imminent, he remain with him, which Custer gladly consented to do.

I described Custer as he appeared when, as a captain, he was with us at Aldie about two weeks before, where, after his ducking, he voluntarily led repeated charges of Kilpatrick's men, attracting the attention of every one present by his conspicuous gallantry. Within that two weeks he, with Farnsworth, Merritt, and Kilpatrick, had been made brigadier-generals. Kilpatrick was given the command of Stahl's division, Farnsworth one of his brigades, and Custer a brigade of four Michigan regiments.

In marked contrast with Custer's costume on the day of the fight at Aldie, he now appeared in a uniform consisting of a black velvet jacket and trousers, with a gold cord on the seam of his trousers and the gilt stripes of a brigadier-general on his arm. He wore a man-o-war's man's shirt with the wide collar out on his shoulders, on each point of which was worked a silver star indicating his rank of brigadier-general. The neck was open, just as a man-o'-war's man has his, and he wore a sailor's tie. On this day he wore a small cap.

It was said at the time, that some months before, soon after he came out of West Point, friends tried to secure for him the colonelcy of the Fifth Michigan cavalry, at this time commanded by Lieutenant-Colonel Russell A. Alger, but, like many volunteers of that period, the men, in their inexperience, preferred officers from the civilians who came out with them, and declined to have Custer. It therefore happened that the man they refused to have as their colonel was sent to be their general, and under his leadership the Michigan cavalry brigade became famous.

The enemy had placed some batteries on our left and front, and advanced from the woods in our front. Colonel McIntosh's brigade met their attacks, a part of his command being dismounted. His entire force soon became hotly engaged, and also the Fifth and Sixth Michigan regiments. General Gregg stationed himself near his batteries, where he could see the field and direct the battle; one of these was Randol's and the other commanded by A. C. M. Pennington, both famous batteries, Randol's to the right and Pennington's to the left. In this engagement the fire of these batteries, especially Pennington's, was remarkably accurate, compelling the enemy at times to shift their guns, and contributed in no small measure to our success.

After the fighting had been in progress for some little time, Custer took off his cap, placed it in his saddle-pocket and led the Seventh Michigan cavalry in a charge, his yellow hair flying and his uniform making him a conspicuous object. The Seventh was a new regiment

Major General George A. Custer

and was armed with a Spencer rifle which carried one cartridge in the barrel and seven in the breech; this was the first time I had seen this weapon. This charge was over a very considerable distance, with the result that the lines were somewhat extended so that when they came close to the enemy behind a fence and were met by a fresh body of Confederate cavalry charging them, they were repulsed.

Being a new regiment, many of the men rode wildly past McIntosh's command and up to and beyond our guns. I think it was during this affair that General Custer's horse was shot. I heard him remark after the fight that he would have been captured except for the fact that one of his buglers caught a horse for him and held off the man who wanted him to surrender. Meanwhile I had been sent to Colonel McIntosh and was with him when the Seventh Michigan men came back past his dismounted lines. He was making heroic efforts to rally them, fairly frothing at the mouth and yelling, "For God's sake, men, if you are ever going to stand, stand now, for you are on your free soil!"

It was just before this that we discovered Stuart's final advance, by Hampton's and Fitz-Hugh Lee's brigades, which Hampton led past McIntosh's dismounted men, charging right up to within about fifty yards of our guns. Believing that, if the guns were taken, there was nothing to prevent the enemy from getting at the reserve artillery and ammunition trains in our rear, it seemed the crisis for us, as it was also about the time Pickett was advancing against the centre of our army's line of battle.

I took a position between two guns, which I think were in charge of Lieutenant Chester, who excited my admiration by his coolness, and there awaited the expected struggle over them. The effect of Pennington's and Randol's firing on Hampton's brigades was soon noticeable, for the momentum of their charge seemed to be checked when they were about one hundred and fifty yards from our guns. Our batteries were then firing canister into them.

Two gallant charges were made into Hampton's columns as they came on. Captain Trichel with about sixteen men of McIntosh's brigade, including Captains Walter Newhall and Rogers, suddenly appeared and charged into them from the right, creating some confusion. Newhall tried to make for a colour-bearer, who lowered his staff, striking him in the mouth, knocked him from his horse, and tore his face open. Trichel, his officers, and nearly all of his men were wounded.

About the same time Captain Miller of the Third Pennsylvania with his company charged right through the rear part of the column from the left. Hampton had led his men to within about fifty yards of Chester's guns, when suddenly the First Michigan cavalry, a veteran and very fine regiment, led by Colonel Towne, with Custer by his side, appeared. The Colonel, in the last stages of consumption it was said, required assistance to mount his horse.

This regiment, which from my position I had not seen, struck the enemy in front and flank, right before our guns, which only then ceased firing. Immediately staff-officers, orderlies, and the men that a moment before had been coming to the rear joined in a hand-to-hand fight in front of the batteries. In a few minutes the enemy broke to the rear and our men, joined by the First New Jersey, Third Pennsylvania, Fifth and Sixth Michigan which had mounted, chased them nearly to the woods from which they had emerged some three quarters of a mile in our front.

This ended General Gregg's cavalry fight at Gettysburg, the fortunate outcome of which undoubtedly contributed greatly to the victory. Immediately word was sent to headquarters of our success and in a short time a brief note was received from, I think, General Butterfield, General Meade's chief of staff, written on a slip of paper about the size of an envelope. The words, as I recall, were: "Congratulations upon your success; attack here repulsed. Longstreet wounded and a prisoner."

The reference to Longstreet was a mistake, Armistead was meant. Riding along the lines I called out the contents of this note to our men, who began cheering, for we then knew that the battle of Gettysburg had been won.

CHAPTER 10

Scenes in Gettysburg

The following morning our burial parties were at work, when a man from a Michigan regiment came and asked me if I would help him look for some of his comrades in a wheat field; the wheat being about three feet high it was not easy to notice a body in it unless one stumbled right on it. In a few minutes he called out that he had found one and then he said he had another. As the burial party was digging a trench on the ridge just beyond, I suggested that he stay where he was to mark the location and I would ride over and get some of the citizens, whom we noticed plundering the battlefield of horse equipments, to help carry the bodies over so they might be buried.

I rode up to two or three men who had harness, saddles, and horse equipments in their possession and told them to drop them and come over to help me carry the bodies that we might bury them, as we had to move on shortly. They were a type of Pennsylvania Dutchmen that lived in that county, who seemed utterly indifferent to the war and anything pertaining to it, beyond securing such spoils as they got on the battle-field. They at once demurred and said they had no time, whereupon I flew into a rage at their heartless conduct, drew my sabre, and threatened to sabre them if they did not come at once. They then sulkily complied. When we got back to where the bodies were I told them to take some fence rails and carry them as though they were a stretcher. We put the bodies across the rails, the men holding the ends of them.

When we had two bodies on this improvised stretcher I discovered a Confederate soldier, a sergeant, with a bushy head of red hair and a red beard. A sabre had split open the top of his head so you could put your hand in the gash. I suggested that he be cared for too, and when we attempted to put him on the stretcher they complained that they could not carry the load. Then I rode after some more citizens whom I also compelled to come over and help us. With their assistance we succeeded in getting a number of bodies up to where the burial party was at work. When I told my Michigan comrade of my experience with these men he became so angry that I thought he would shoot them then and there.

The general then moved into the town of Gettysburg, where, in contrast to the heartless conduct of these men, we found patriotic women at work in every house pulling lint and doing what they could to alleviate the suffering that was all around them. One lady, who, I was told, was the wife of a physician killed on the Peninsula, came out on the front porch and asked every soldier she saw to come in and have hot coffee and biscuit. The men gave her coffee, which she made in a wash-boiler, but the biscuits were made from flour she possessed, which by this time was about exhausted.

As it was likely to be several days before normal conditions could be restored in the town, I suggested that she had better cease baking biscuits and save the little flour she had for her family, when she replied that she would take the chance, that as long as she had any she was going to give it to the soldiers.

About this time Nick, the general's bugler, came to me and reported that he had found a citizen who had fought with our troops and been wounded, an old man, and Nick wanted a doctor to go and see him as he was in his own house nearby. This citizen proved to be the famous John Burns, an old man of seventy, who fought, I think with a Wisconsin regiment. Whether anybody else had discovered Burns before Nick did I am not sure, but my recollection is that Nick's discovery first called the attention of our people to the fact.

General Gregg's command then moved out on the Chambersburg pike, where for miles we saw the distressing evidences of the battle in the shape of the Confederate wounded, who were in every barn and building and lying beside the road. It had rained heavily the night before and the fields in which these men lay were flooded with water. Those able to do so had secured rails, upon which their helpless comrades were placed to keep them out of the water. I think the division that day captured, including the wounded, about four thousand.

General Gregg sent back a report of the condition of these poor Confederate wounded whom Lee had been obliged to leave behind, and asked that ambulances be sent out to take them in where they could have the attention of our surgeons, then overworked and exhausted caring for the thousands of wounded among our own men.

From Chambersburg we marched back to Gettysburg and thence to Boonesborough, arriving there about the ninth. In the neighbourhood of Boonesborough we met the Seventh New York militia, whose fine band of about sixty pieces, led by Graffula, that night serenaded General Meade. The square in front of his headquarters was thronged with men listening to the fine music, the like of which we never heard in the army. One man, I think from Indiana, remarked to me: "I tell ye the bullet hain't run that will kill a fellow when that band's a-playin'."

CHAPTER 11

Return to Virginia

Within a few days General Gregg was directed to cross the Potomac at Harper's Ferry and move out to the vicinity of the road leading from Martinsburg to Winchester, which was General Lee's line of communications, to do what was possible to cripple his wagon trains. We moved through Charlestown and the next day reached Shepherdstown, where the Confederates had large stores of provisions. The people there were divided in sentiment, some sympathizing with the South, and a few with the Union army. With a view of rewarding the Union sympathizers, some of us took flour and bacon from the Confederate stores and presented it to the families that we believed to be in sympathy with the Union, to the disgust of those who favoured the South.

This proved to be an unfortunate performance on our part for the recipients of our favours. While this was going on the enemy attacked and drove in our pickets and advanced in force. Fortunately the First Maine cavalry was mounted and on the road, going out for forage. Colonel Smith, their commander, at once deployed his regiment and checked the rapid advance of the enemy until General Gregg could get out the rest of the command and occupy a good position.

That morning some prisoners were brought in and as they were taking a squad to the rear I asked one of the men what regiment he belonged to. Upon his reply that it was the Twenty-eighth Louisiana and that it was from New Orleans, I asked him if he knew any one by the name of Sykes. He inquired if he was one of the auctioneer's sons. On telling him he was, he replied that they had two in his regiment and that one of them had been wounded and left back at some place, which I do not now recall. This Sykes was a second cousin of mine.

On writing home I reported the circumstance to my mother,

whose brother, my uncle, shortly after visited New Orleans and was thus able to give information to Sykes's mother in New Orleans regarding her son, she up to that time having had no word as to his whereabouts or condition. He subsequently recovered.

About this time General Gregg received word that Lee's army had entirely recrossed the Potomac, so it was too late to accomplish anything with two brigades. He also found that they were moving around to surround us, as several couriers were captured on the way from Harper's Ferry, the main roads leading there then being occupied by the enemy. General Gregg, as usual under such conditions, made a splendid fight, the enemy making repeated efforts to drive us, but were every time repulsed by Irwin Gregg's brigade and the fire of our battery. They kept up their attacks until dark.

That night the wounded who could be moved were started back for Harper's Ferry by a road close to the river's edge, the only one not occupied by the enemy, the General and his staff leaving some time after midnight, and our rearguard about daylight. Within due time we reached Harper's Ferry with no losses other than the killed and those so badly wounded that we were unable to move them. These were left in a church with a surgeon and the ladies of Shepherdstown, who were zealous in their efforts to assist in alleviating the suffering of our men.

During August and September, the division was kept busy watching the movements of the enemy. Several skirmishes and engagements occurred. The most notable that I recall was one during the advance from Sulphur Springs to Culpeper and thence to the Rapidan, which I think was in September. Kilpatrick's division came by way of Brandy Station while we moved from Sulphur Springs, the two divisions meeting about midday at Culpeper. After stopping to feed, the advance was resumed when, just beyond that town, the enemy made a sharp counter attack, but we finally, when our reserves were brought up, drove them back.

Later in the day we went into camp in an abandoned cornfield, when it began to rain and we remained there in the rain for I think forty-eight hours. Indeed, my clothing had been wet through for probably sixty hours, because on the morning of the advance before we arrived at Culpeper we reached a bridge which the enemy had set fire to, thus temporarily checking our advance. As the general rode up some of our men were pulling off the plank. I noticed that this would not save the bridge, since the combustible material was suspended from below. Riding into the stream and under the bridge I began pulling down the burning material thus suspended, others following and helping me, and within a few minutes we had the fire out, the planks restored, and, with our mounted men fording the stream, we were able to take our artillery across, when the enemy fell back.

As we were liable at any moment to meet with a counter charge, I was afraid to take time to get off my horse and take my long cavalry boots off to pour the water out of them, consequently I rode with about half a pail of water in each boot-leg for a good part of the day. This fact and the rain coming on later was the reason why my clothing was wet for the period mentioned. No ill results, however, followed this, for when the sun finally came out my clothes were soon dry.

CHAPTER 12

Battle at Buckland's Mills

The following September General Kilpatrick, having become commander of a division in July previous, applied to have me ordered to my regiment in his division in order that I might be detailed for duty at his headquarters. General Gregg wrote a letter to General Pleasanton, the corps commander, requesting a "suspension of the order," because of the absence, by reason of illness, of his adjutant-general, Captain Weir, in which he stated substantially that he had no staff-officers familiar with the adjutant-general's duties and that my services were then "invaluable to him."[1]

The order was thereupon suspended until Captain Weir's return, when I reported to General Kilpatrick. About this time, Captain Weir recommended me for a commission, which recommendation was endorsed by General Gregg.[2] I was very sorry to leave General Gregg's headquarters, for I had come to have great admiration for him and Captain Weir, both as soldiers and high-toned, patriotic men.

At General Kilpatrick's headquarters I performed the same duties as at General Gregg's, acting largely in the capacity of private secretary to him when in camp, and doing a staff-officer's duty in the field, until the following February. I was present with him at all the engagements the division took part in during that period; the most important of which that I recall was on the retreat from Culpeper, and later at Buckland's Mills near Warrenton, about October 20th. The former was on the occasion of the retirement from Culpeper and Brandy Station.

After leaving Culpeper General Custer's brigade had the advance and General H. E. Davies, Jr., was covering the rear. General Pleasan-

1. See Appendix B.
2. *Ibid*

ton, the corps commander, and his staff and escort happened to be riding near General Kilpatrick and his staff, and Custer with three regiments was, I think, in column of squadrons moving on the open plain between Culpeper and Brandy Station and to the left of the railroad. The wagons of the two brigades were in the advance, as we were retiring.

It was a bright October afternoon and one could see for a considerable distance ahead. A stream called Mountain Run had to be crossed and we noticed confusion at it, though it was probably a mile ahead. Presently someone appeared and reported that the enemy were in position directly across our line of march on the opposite side of the run. To their left they had a battery which had the range of the little bridge over which our entire column must pass to cross Mountain Run. It thus seemed that we were likely to be cut off and the only alternative was to charge right through this force directly in our front. Kilpatrick gave orders to Custer to charge with his entire command and we then advanced in practically five columns. This was a fine sight and a thrilling moment. Pleasanton's staff and escort, Kilpatrick's staff and escort, and Custer's three or four regiments.

When we arrived within a reasonable charging distance of the enemy posted as I have described, Custer ordered his band to strike up *Yankee Doodle*; the men on hearing this began cheering when the bugle sounded the charge. The five columns rushed forward and the enemy broke before we reached them, moving into the woods on their left and our right, across the railroad. I remember one gallant Confederate riding out in an effort to rally their men, standing in plain sight with his battle-flag stuck in the ground, holding it off from his horse at arm's length, but it was of no use, and he finally was obliged to retire.

Meanwhile the enemy appeared on our left and rear, and part of our force had to turn and meet them, Davies, who was covering our rear, being also strongly pressed as he was retiring from Culpeper. Repeated charges were made and the enemy held back until our wagons, ambulances, and artillery were gotten over the little bridge previously referred to at Mountain Run. Ultimately the entire command crossed at this point. The enemy had such an accurate range of this crossing-place that they dropped their shells on and in the immediate vicinity of the bridge during the crossing of our men.

Just as I passed it, the man who was riding ahead of me, whose horse mine could touch, had his head taken off by a shell just as

Brevet Brigadier General E. W. Whitaker

though it had been severed by an axe; the remarkable fact was that his headless body remained straight in the saddle for an instant or two, finally toppling over. When we reached Brandy Station we made a junction with Buford's command, which we found had been coming up in rear of the line that was drawn up to cut us off. This doubtless had something to do with their breaking before we reached them in the charge I have described. We then crossed the Rappahannock and camped for the night. This was the third engagement that I had been in at Brandy Station.

On October 19th occurred the engagement at Buckland's Mills, near Warrenton. In this Kilpatrick's command was defeated. In the advance toward Warrenton there was an interval of about two miles between General Davies's brigade, which had the advance, and General Custer's. We had been driving the enemy during the morning toward Warrenton, and had halted to feed when a force of the enemy came unexpectedly in between Custer's and Davies's brigades, overwhelmed General Custer's command, and drove it back across Broad Run; and by taking possession of the bridge and the Warrenton pike, had cut off General Davies's command, which was then vigorously attacked by Hampton's force, which Davies had been pushing toward Warrenton up to this time.

Kilpatrick, when he found Custer was thus attacked, had sent one or two staff-officers to Davies with orders for him to fall back and make a junction with Custer. These apparently were unable to reach him, and Kilpatrick, when he found that Custer could not hold his position, became very anxious that word should be gotten to Davies of the real situation and the danger that his brigade might be cut off and a large portion of them captured. As he crossed the bridge with the rear of Custer's command he turned to me, as I was riding near him, no staff-officer being at the moment about, and remarked: "Meyer, somebody must get to Davies and let him know that Custer has been driven across Broad Run and that the enemy have got this bridge."

On turning my horse to go back, he called out: "Tell him to make his way the best he can to Haymarket where he will find General Newton's corps."

I was unable to return across the bridge, as the enemy had the other end of it and were moving up the stream so as to intercept Davies, whom they knew was being driven back on them. Riding until beyond their line I saw some of Custer's men, who had been cut off, come out of the woods at that point and cross the stream to escape, when I took advantage of the confusion to cross to the west side, trusting I would not be noticed and that the woods at that point would screen me from observation. Being familiar with the country I made my way around their flank and rear, having the sound of Davies's firing to direct me to his whereabouts. I soon reached him and found him hard pressed. When I reported the situation, his men were rallied for another charge, which was led by Captain J. F. B. Mitchell, so as to gain time to permit a withdrawal, as directed. We then galloped across the country, the forces opposing following on our flanks, until we crossed Broad Run farther up towards Haymarket. Davies's artillery had meanwhile been conducted away in safety under the guidance of Doctor Capehart, of the First West Virginia cavalry, who knew the country well. The brigade was thus saved from serious loss; indeed, none other than the casualties in fighting. Custer's and Davies's brigades formed a junction when they reached the First Corps commanded by General Newton, and the enemy withdrew.

General Kilpatrick was quite chagrined that evening over the surprise his command had been subjected to and the defeat it met, and claimed that he never would have separated Davies's and Custer's brigades and given the enemy a chance to get in between them by means of the road from Auburn through the woods, had he not supposed that this road was being looked after by someone else, whose name I do not now recall.

Custer's command, which was feeding when attacked, made a gallant fight under very great disadvantages. The remarkably accurate firing by Pennington's battery, however, checked the enemy's advance and Custer's personal efforts saved his brigade from much greater losses. Stuart, the Confederate commander, in his report, claimed that it was "the greatest rout that any cavalry had suffered during the war," and the Richmond papers described the fight as the "Buckland Races." This I think is an exaggerated statement. Of course we were defeated, but as soon as Custer got across the stream his men were rallied and as fit to take the offensive as they were in the morning. Davies's brigade fought gallantly to resist Hampton's assaults, which began as soon as the firing on Custer in the rear was heard. It was only after I gave Davies the information that Custer had been driven across Broad Run and that the enemy had the bridge and were in his rear, moving towards Haymarket to intercept him, that he started his command on the gallop across the country to that village. When he had made a

CAPTAIN THEODORE F. NORTHROP

junction with Custer, both brigades were ready to take the offensive; at any rate the enemy withdrew.

An amusing incident that occurred after Custer's men had gotten over Broad Run and were being rallied was told me, to the effect that an Irishman rode up to Kilpatrick, who was riding his horse called "Spot," a speckled roan with a white rump, saying: "I say, 'Kil,' stop here, and the boys will see your horse and they will rally round you, so they will." This the general did, resulting as the Irishman had predicted.

In December General Custer was temporarily in command of the division, and on his recommendation I was allowed a furlough of ten days. During that ten days I dined one evening with Admiral Hiram Paulding, then in command of the Brooklyn Navy Yard. (His son had been a schoolmate and the admiral had known me before the war.) He questioned me as to my position in the field, and expressed considerable surprise when I told him I was not a commissioned officer, and quite embarrassed me, as there were a number of prominent officers at the table, by slapping me on the back and in a loud voice, to attract the attention of all present, stating that he was proud to sit alongside of a private soldier of the United States Army, and a gentleman.

He then asked me to call upon him the next morning, when he gave me a letter addressed to the Hon. John Potts, the chief clerk of the War Department and an old friend of his, which recommended me for a commission. I never presented this letter,[3] however. He subsequently wrote letters[4] to Governor Seymour, and Adjutant-General D. Townsend, U. S. A., copies of which he gave me, and to General Kilpatrick. General Kilpatrick later gave me a copy of the one he received.[5]

About this time, General Kilpatrick, hearing that my friends at home had interested themselves in the matter of procuring me a commission, wrote a letter to the Hon. George T. Cobb, an influential member of Congress from New Jersey, a copy of which Captain L. G. Estes, his adjutant-general, gave me.[6] In February an order from the War Department discharging me as a private from the Harris Light Cavalry to accept a commission in the Twenty-fourth New York Cavalry was received at General Kilpatrick's headquarters at Stevensburg. I did not care to leave the general and went to him for advice; yet the idea of going home on a furlough with promotion was quite attrac-

---

3, 4, 5, 6. See Appendix B.

tive, and the general told me that he thought, on the whole, promotion in a new regiment was more apt to be rapid since there would be a good many changes during the first campaign, and, "in any event," he remarked, "if your regiment comes anywhere near where I am I will have you detailed on my staff." Thanking the general and bidding him and my friends goodbye, I left his headquarters for my new field of duty.

Brevet Brigadier General L. G. Estes

CHAPTER 13

At Camp Stoneman

I returned to New York, procured my uniform, and immediately reported at Auburn, where the Twenty-fourth Cavalry was rendezvoused. To my surprise, I found that they were under orders to proceed at once to Washington. When I reported to Colonel Raulston, commanding, he told me that he proposed to assign me to Company D, as this company had no captain, and he did not think the first lieutenant, who had recruited most of the men, was likely to remain long in the service and was unable to enforce the necessary discipline. Though I was a second lieutenant, he expected to hold me responsible for the safe conduct of the men to Washington and the drilling and care of the company.

It seems that the first lieutenant, who was a well-meaning man, was not suited for military life; he did not realize what was required and expected of him, was incapable of securing the confidence of the men, and totally ignorant of the duties of a company commander; and consequently with his concurrence and with perfect good feeling between us, I took charge of the company, drilled them, and had practically charge of them until compelled to leave them by reason of wounds, as will be explained later.

The regiment left Auburn for Washington *via* Elmira and Baltimore. It rode in passenger-cars from Auburn to Elmira, and at Elmira, notwithstanding the season of the year, February, the regiment was placed in freight-cars and was thus transported to Baltimore. As the men had received large bounties I was, I assume, in common with the other company commanders, told that I would be held responsible should any of my men desert while *en route* to Washington.

The train made frequent stops and was held at stations to allow other traffic to pass, and I think we were something like forty-eight hours *en route*. It seemed to me hard to keep the men cramped up in these cars in which they simply had planks to sit on, so I told them that at each station we stopped at I would allow a certain number to get out and take a little exercise, but that in accepting this privilege if any of them took advantage of it to desert I would have to suffer for it, yet I would take the chances that they would be fair to me. This they were, since none of them deserted.

Before reaching Baltimore an amusing incident occurred that illustrates a volunteer soldier's idea of discipline on joining the army. At one of the stopping-places where my men were out walking on the platform, Lieutenant-Colonel Newberry remarked that he noticed my men out at every station, intimating that I was not holding them well in hand. I replied that I thought it a hardship not to let them take some exercise, the weather being cold, but that if he directed me not to allow them to leave the cars I would carry out his instructions. At this he turned and made no reply. A couple of Irishmen of my company overheard the conversation, one of whom exclaimed: "I say, Lieutenant, if you say the word we will belt hell out of him, so we will!" Ordering the men to get in the car, I had great difficulty to refrain from laughing.

If the colonel heard the remark he doubtless was amused at it; at any rate he ignored it. He had a keen sense of the ludicrous, and no officer could be more considerate of his men than he subsequently proved to be. When the train conveying the regiment reached Baltimore, the sides of many of the cars had been stripped of their covering, which had been used to make fires *en route*. We finally reached the old Baltimore and Ohio station in Washington at night, it being very cold. From there we marched to Camp Stoneman, a cavalry camp of instruction across Potomac Creek, where the regiment was drilled and put in shape for the campaign that began in May.

Having had experience in a cavalry regiment and being familiar with cavalry tactics, and also with the various details of camp duties, I was able to suggest how my inexperienced men could be comfortable in camp, as soon as we reached Camp Stoneman. The regiment was, in May, assigned to Burnside's Ninth Corps, and joined the Army of the Potomac, after a hard day's march, the afternoon of the second day of the battle of the Wilderness.

As soon as our regiment advanced into the woods, I was selected to take command of a skirmish line that was to cover, as I remember, the front of our brigade. I assumed that I was selected for this duty,

Colonel William C. Raulston

though only a second lieutenant in rank, because of the fact of my prior service with the Harris Light Cavalry and with Generals Gregg and Kilpatrick. Nothing serious occurred, however, to my command that day.

On the evening of the last day of the battle of the Wilderness we built a new line of breastworks, which were in close proximity to the enemy's lines. With a view to sparing my men, who were then much exhausted, I had the works in my front built by stragglers from other regiments, of whom there were a large number, releasing them when the work was finished. At dark, in order to prevent a surprise, as it was extremely difficult to keep the men awake, we placed a line of pickets about fifty yards outside of our works. A short time after, someone on our line fired a shot, when immediately the whole line arose and began shooting. Believing that it was a false alarm, I jumped up to look over the breastworks to see if I could see any firing from the enemy's lines.

At that moment I heard our pickets outside, who were subjected to this fire, calling out, "For God's sake stop firing, you are killing your own men!" Running along the line giving orders to stop the firing, I had a narrow escape from one excited fellow who fired his carbine off, the muzzle of which was close to my ear as I was in the act of grabbing another man who, in his excitement, was about to shoot. The line, however, soon quieted down.

Presently a messenger came to me and speaking in a low tone directed me to keep a sharp lookout and when I saw the troops on my right move, to have my men follow as noiselessly as possible, and he enjoined me to see that the men carried their canteens and tin cups in their hands in order that no noise might be heard by the enemy whose lines were so close by. I was soon notified, "They are moving." Quickly walking along the line I awoke the men and cautioned them to be as quiet as possible. In this manner we moved out and for some moments were in suspense lest the enemy hear the movement and, by attacking, stop it.

After a while we reached a place where we could form in column of fours, and all that night we marched through narrow roads in the woods of that region, halting every few minutes because of obstructions due to teams and other troops in our front. This fatiguing process continued until about daylight, when we reached the main road where the country was open. We were all greatly depressed, since after the three days' desperate fighting at the Wilderness no apparent

71

advantage had been gained, and we assumed that the army had been unsuccessful and that it was an attempt to retreat.

We soon came to a house outside of which I saw a coloured woman apparently dressed up, since it was Sunday. I called out to her and asked what road we were marching on. Upon hearing her reply, "The road to Spottsylvania Court House," a thrill of satisfaction instantly passed through every man in the column, since then we realized that we at last had a general and that our movement was south and towards the rear of Lee's army. From that time until the end of my service I never had any misgiving as to Grant's capacity to lead us to final victory.

It was on this morning that I first saw General Grant. The road ahead was blocked and our men were lying in it when someone called out, "Get your men to one side to allow General Grant to pass." Grant, however, gave directions not to disturb the tired men, many of whom were asleep, and turned into a field. We were all up, however, anxious to see him. He appeared riding a small black horse with his feet not more than two feet from the ground. He had a couple of staff-officers with him, one of whom was Captain Parker, an Indian, and an orderly. His unpretentious appearance excited the comment of all, and had we not been told who he was he would have attracted no more attention than an ordinary line officer.

CHAPTER 14

Sent to Washington for Ammunition

A little after noon the regiment reached a position in the vicinity of Spottsylvania, where details of men were given me and I was instructed to go into the woods and establish a line of skirmishers in a favourable location. We found the underbrush in these woods on fire, so using a portion of the men to beat out the fire I placed the remainder on a line which we occupied until the next day, when we were moved to another part of the field. It was so difficult to keep my men awake that, in order to avoid a surprise, I went along the line at frequent intervals during the night, sometimes being obliged to wake up some of them.

While in front of Spottsylvania Court House I was in command of a force that held the line of works on the road to that town. We were under fire most of the day until, towards evening, the enemy retired. With the desire to have my men get a little refreshment, I suggested that some part of the men cook coffee while the others remained in the trenches in line. There being no firewood I suggested that some rails be pulled out of a breastwork that ran at right angles to one that we had been occupying. On lifting these rails a man reported that he saw the body of a Confederate soldier in the breastworks. I then had a considerable portion of the breastworks uncovered, and found that they had placed in them a number of dead Confederates and piled rails and dirt on top of them, thus forming the breastwork behind which they had fought. Reporting this on being relieved, I saw it afterward commented on in some of the Northern papers.

It will be remembered that the battle of Spottsylvania was a very sanguinary one, the enemy being strongly posted behind breastworks in a rough-wooded country, and the assaults made on these works had cost our army a loss of nearly twenty thousand men, killed and wounded. A night or two before the army moved from there, I was called from my place in the line of breastworks and directed to report at division headquarters. On arriving there I was introduced to an officer who, I was told, was a topographical engineer from army headquarters, and that I was to go with him.

It was a dark night with a drizzling rain falling. As we mounted our horses he told me that I was selected to conduct a division later in the night to a position from which they were to assault the enemy's works, the attack to be made before daylight, hoping to surprise them, previous assaults in the daytime having proved so disastrous to our men. He stated that he wanted to have me familiarize myself thoroughly with the ground where the division was to be placed in position for the charge so that I could explain it to the general in command, and thus avoid a chance of confusion among the troops and failure of the attack.

On hearing what was expected of me I was naturally greatly impressed with the responsibility, fearing that if I made a mistake it might be very disastrous in its results. We soon reached a small corduroy bridge, about wide enough for a column of fours to cross, from which a roadway passed through a piece of woods, as I remember it, a few rods, to a clearing. We left our horses with our orderlies at this bridge and walked till we came to the clearing. He told me that a few rods in front the ground began to ascend, and farther up on this slope was the line of works the division was to attack and attempt to surprise. He then walked with me along the clearing to the right, explaining about how many yards it extended in that direction from the opening by which we had entered, and told me about how many could be placed in line there.

We then returned to the opening and walked to the left of it, where he explained about how many men could be placed there. On our return to this road, I suggested that we had better move up the hill a little more so that I could familiarize myself with the character of the ground over which the assault was to be made. This was done and we lay on the ground where we could hear sounds from the enemy's lines. We then returned to our horses. In my anxiety not to make a mistake, I suggested that we go all over it again and that he let me show him the way in the manner I was expected to direct the general, to make sure that I correctly understood what I was to do. He assented to this, and at its conclusion expressed himself as satisfied that I understood the duty assigned to me.

On the ride back to headquarters I think nothing was said. I was naturally thinking over what would be the result of this night attack and wondering whether I would ever see daylight again. Reaching headquarters, this officer, whose name I never learned and whose face I could not even recall, as it was dark the entire time I was with him, told me I had better lie down and get a little sleep and that I would be called when wanted. Then taking me by the hand he said, "Goodbye and God bless you!" and withdrew.

When I awoke the sun was up, and upon inquiry I was informed that about two o'clock in the morning a message was received from headquarters countermanding the order for the assault. After the war, I read in some of General Grant's writings that after assenting to this proposed assault he was awake in his tent thinking over the prospects of its success and decided that the chances in the darkness were against it. Therefore, soon after midnight, he directed that the order for it be countermanded. I assume that the contemplated assault was to include other troops than the division I was detailed to accompany.

One night, while with my company in the breastworks, I was sent for and informed by Colonel Raulston that General Burnside had requested him to recommend an officer whom he could send to Washington to bring back with him, at the earliest possible moment, some carbine ammunition for our regiment, it being of a different calibre from that used by the other regiments of the division, which were infantry. Colonel Raulston told me he had decided to detail me for this duty and directed me to report to General Burnside. I rode to the latter's headquarters, where he gave me a letter to the War Department and one addressed to his wife. The latter he requested me to mail in Washington, mail communication with the army at that time having been temporarily cut off.

I started immediately in a dense fog for Belle Plain, riding all night, and was obliged to procure a fresh horse in the morning at Fredericksburg. I sailed from Belle Plain for Washington, arriving the next morning, and as soon as the War Department opened for business I presented my letters, and was informed that the necessary ammunition would be placed on a tug which would be ready to sail for Belle Plain that afternoon.

I was told that a permit had been given to the late Bishop McIlvaine, of Ohio, and George H. Stuart, the president of the Christian Commission, to go on the boat with me, they having been granted permission to go to the front to look into the practical working of the

United States Christian Commission. When the tug sailed, I being the only United States officer or soldier on board, Mr. Stuart introduced himself to me, and then presented me to the Bishop.

Later he came to me and said that it was proposed to have a brief prayer-meeting in the cabin, at which were present the Bishop, Mr. Stuart, and one or two representatives of the Christian Commission, and a lady, who, I was told, had a pass from Mr. Lincoln permitting her to go to the front to see her son, who was wounded. It impressed me as an exceedingly pathetic and remarkable incident, and I remember that, being brought up a Presbyterian, I was a little curious to see whether the Bishop would read his prayers from the prayer-book or would make one extemporaneously. He, however, made what seemed to me then one of the most affecting and beautiful extempore prayers I ever listened to.

When the little steamboat reached Belle Plain, the Bishop's party were put into an ambulance and had an escort of a part of a regiment to take them to Fredericksburg, as the intervening country was raided by Mosby's men and all wagon trains between Belle Plain and Fredericksburg had to be heavily guarded.

No transportation being provided for me to take my ammunition to the front, I took the responsibility of taking some wagons belonging to General Potter's division, none of my own being available. I did this without authority, but under stress of circumstances. When I got them loaded I found it was impossible to start that afternoon, as no escort could be furnished until the next morning. I concluded, however, the general would be anxious to know that the ammunition was *en route*, and I decided to start on alone for Fredericksburg. Putting my pistol in my boot-leg, I started off in a very severe thunder-storm, and, keeping a good lookout, rode to Fredericksburg without meeting any of the enemy's roving cavalry.

That night I spent with Captain Corson, quartermaster of General Gregg's division at Fredericksburg, and started the next morning for the front, where I reported to General Crittenden when he might expect the first wagons containing the ammunition, and then rode back to Fredericksburg to hurry them forward. When I returned with the first two wagons the regiment was in action, and I was obliged to get details of men to break open the boxes and carry the cartridges in blankets to supply the men along the line.

I remember being verbally complimented for getting back some twelve hours sooner than it was thought possible, and shortly afterwards General Crittenden detailed me on his staff, but I declined the position, as my men expected me to stay with them and I had intimated that I would stay with them through the campaign. It was a few days after this that I was commissioned captain.

I might add that I understood General Potter was very angry, as he needed his wagons to bring commissary stores for his troops, and proposed to prefer charges against me for unwarrantably taking them. If he did so, I never heard anything from it. I took for granted that the necessities of the case justified my action.

CHAPTER 15

Wounded

From Spottsylvania, until the army reached Petersburg, some portion of the regiment was under fire every day. During this period occurred the engagements at the North Anna River, Pamunkey, and Cold Harbor. The most fatiguing march that I ever experienced was that made by our brigade on its withdrawal from the south bank of the North Anna River, in which we had a similar experience to that during the withdrawal from the lines at the Wilderness, the men realizing that if we were attacked then it would be on the brink of a rapid running river we were about to recross. We crossed the North Anna River sometime between darkness and midnight, and then moved by a circuitous route, as the more direct lines were occupied by other troops.

We marched, without any halts other than those occasioned by blockades ahead of us, all the next day and following night. In order to prevent my tired men from falling out, and not having the heart to urge them to keep up while I was riding my horse, I dismounted and walked at the rear of the company, feeling that so long as I was able to walk I could with propriety urge the men to do likewise. It was reported at the time that some of our men died of exhaustion in the middle of the night; at any rate, when the command finally halted and stacked arms fully one half of it were not able to answer the roll-call. During the following twenty-four hours, however, our stragglers kept coming in.

In a day or two the battle of Cold Harbor occurred. Our regiment went into line in an unfavourable position, it being in an abandoned cornfield, the woods beyond being held by the enemy. As was the custom whenever we went into line at night to throw up temporary breastworks, we were directed to do so here. The soil was sandy, there were no timber and no rail fences, and we had few intrenching tools, consequently it seemed impossible with the facilities at hand to construct any sort of temporary breastworks. Within a few rods of my company's position in the lines stood a large house, from which the family had hastily departed.

As there was no timber, the only alternative that suggested itself to me was to take the roof from the house and break it up for our purpose. I therefore sent a detail of men who in a short time removed the roof from this building, while others soon knocked down the rest of the structure. This material was broken up, the sand piled on it, and thus were provided the breastworks that protected us the next day. This seemed a hardship to the occupants of this dwelling, but it was justified by the circumstances.

During the battle of Cold Harbor I had a second opportunity to see General Grant, having been sent to General Meade's headquarters where General Grant happened to be. When I reached headquarters, I found General Meade sprawled out on the ground with his face buried in a map, he being very near-sighted. Staff-officers were constantly riding up and reporting, and about fifty feet from where he lay I saw General Grant sitting alone on a stretcher. He had nothing to say to any one and seemed unconcerned.

While waiting for my instructions, I intently watched him. Presently an officer brought up a Confederate officer, who was a prisoner. Looking up, General Grant quietly asked, "I assume you have questioned him?"

The officer replied, "Yes, but he does not tell anything."

Grant then remarked, "Ask him if he has a recent Richmond paper."

The Confederate officer said that he had and took one from his haversack, giving it to the officer, who handed it to General Grant. Grant nodded his head in acknowledgment, and remarking, "You may take him back," opened the paper and began to read.

Just then General Sheridan rode up. Grant arose, greeted him warmly, and seemed deeply interested as Sheridan began earnestly telling him, I assume, the results of his recent movements. Receiving my instructions I then returned to the regiment.

The crossing of the James River by the army on pontoon bridges, as is known, was a memorable movement, the river being about two thousand feet wide there. Our march from the James River to Petersburg was a very hard one, since the roads were sandy and it seemed that at every two steps forward we would slip one backward. However, towards evening, we reached a position near Petersburg, when, tired as we were, it seemed to me a favourable moment for us to advance and try to capture the town. We could see trains of cars coming in, their infantry being hastily unloaded, and everywhere were evidences that they were hurrying up forces to resist us.

The failure to attack that afternoon was a great disappointment to General Grant, as one reading his *Memoirs* can ascertain. The next day, the 17th of June, was my last day of active service in the field.

About the 8th or 9th of June orders had been read out behind the breastworks in which my appointment as captain was announced. Though I had always been doing duty as a captain, I had never held the rank of a first-lieutenant. Subsequently, Adjutant Hill having been wounded, I did temporary duty as adjutant; and on the 17th of June was with the regiment in the assault of the enemy's works near the Norfolk road, in which it suffered so severely.

My wound was not received in the assault but immediately after, and under the following circumstances. The assault had been unsuccessful because of the failure of some troops on our right to support us properly, and the command had secured the protection of a line of breastworks. Acting as adjutant that day I had been carrying an order, when I noticed lying on the field Lieutenant Randall, who was lying on his face, and about him were our killed and wounded, among others, General Morton, General Burnside's chief engineer.

I turned back to see if Randall was alive, and found him lying with his face buried in the dirt of a corn-hill, the field being a succession of ridges, and the corn being about eighteen inches high. He had a hole in his neck and was apparently dying. I brushed the dirt out of his face so that he could breathe, propped him up on the dirt ridges, but was unable to carry him into our lines, because I had been suffering for some days from intermittent fever and was almost too weak to walk when I went into the engagement. While thus stooping over and in the act of starting for our lines, a ball struck me alongside of the spine, just above my sabre belt, and, as afterwards turned out, ploughed up in the neighborhood of my shoulders.

Realizing that I was struck in a bad place and not wishing to lie there in the sun during the afternoon, I started for our breastworks, the bullets striking the ground around me as I crawled. I asked a man who I believed belonged to the Eighteenth Corps if he could pull me over, as I was unable to get over. He remarked, "I will, if my partner will help me," and in a moment these two men jumped upon the breastwork, took me by the collar of my cavalry jacket, jerked me over, and dropped me inside.

It had not occurred to me that I was in plain sight of the enemy, and it was not until after I was lifting Randall that I noticed the bullets were striking in the ground around me and subsequently in the breastworks, as I lay outside of them, when I asked the man to help me over.

Just after I was pulled over, General Walter C. Newberry, then the lieutenant-colonel of the Twenty-fourth cavalry, who that day commanded the regiment, came up to me. I showed him my wound and remarked that I thought I had a "thirty-day wound." He sent two men who lifted me on my feet, and, with my arm about their necks and their arms supporting my body, I walked a considerable distance before I could reach an ambulance, which took me to the field hospital.

On my way to the field hospital I noticed a corporal, Frederick Gundlach, a brave and honest soldier, who was walking holding his hand, which seemed to be shattered. I hailed him and he immediately ran along by the ambulance in which I was, stayed by me, and waited on me during the afternoon and night. During the night I was placed in a tent with five other seriously wounded officers, including Colonel Raulston of the Twenty-fourth and Captain Burch, the latter dying in the arms of his men as he lay directly opposite me in the tent, During the night it was reported to us that an officer outside had been obliged to have his clothing cut off to get at his wounds, as he had five bullets in his body, in various places, and a blanket was wanted to put around him.

As Corporal Gundlach had given me his blanket to lie on and my overcoat was wrapped around my sabre hilt and pistol, so as to make a pillow for me, I gave them the coat to wrap around this badly wounded man, who proved to be none other than the Lieutenant Randall that I had assisted when I received my wound. It was assumed that by brushing the dirt out of his face and turning him over so he could breathe, he regained consciousness, and when the enemy's position was taken in a later assault that afternoon, he, with the other wounded, was brought in. At any rate, he lived several years after the war, though I never met him again.[1]

---

1. After the war, a medal of honour was awarded to me on the recommendation of General Newberry; see correspondence in Appendix A.

The day after I was wounded I am unable to account for. I may have been insensible; at any rate, it was the second day after, that the ambulances and army wagons were filled with wounded and started for City Point, whence steamboats conveyed them to Washington. I was fortunate in being placed in an ambulance with another badly wounded officer, as these vehicles had springs, while many of the wounded had to ride in the army wagons that had none, hence when going downhill or over rough roads the jolting caused great suffering.

A whole day was consumed in making the trip to City Point, delays constantly occurring because we had to pull out beside the road to permit supply and ammunition wagons to pass, it being the custom in war always to give the right of way to supplies for the front. The heat and the dust settling down on us made it a very trying day, and when the teams reached City Point a number of the wounded were found dead.

We were placed on a large steamboat, where the cots were arranged on the decks as near together as they could be placed and permit nurses to pass between them. These were clean and there was an abundance of food and drink for those able to partake of it. We were on this steamboat that night and the following day, reaching the wharf at the foot of Sixth Street in Washington about sundown.

By this time I was suffering considerably. Because of the nature of my wound I was the last man removed from the boat, it then being nine o'clock. It was decided that the best way to handle me was to carry me on the mattress, so a number of men held it over the stairwell, as I was on the upper deck, while others took it from below. The journey in an ambulance through the streets of Washington, then not paved, was a painful one. I finally reached the Seminary Hospital at Georgetown, where I was bathed and my soiled clothing replaced by clean linen, and placed in a comfortable cot which I occupied for nearly four months.

There were, during that period, usually six wounded officers in the room at a time. Dr. Ducachet was the surgeon-in-chief and Dr. Finn the assistant surgeon; the latter had charge of me. He took good care of me, and I am doubtless greatly indebted to him for my recovery. For three weeks repeated attempts were made to find the ball by probing, but without success. One day a large swelling appeared on my back, and in turning me over in bed to dress the wound a sudden discharge occurred with great force, whereupon the surgeons were summoned

BREVET BRIGADIER GENERAL WALTER C. NEWBERRY

and concluded that this violent discharge must have forced the ball from its lodgment, which had been beyond the reach of their longest probe, and it was decided to attempt to get the ball out.

After sundown, when the day was cooler, the weather at that time being excessively hot, the operation was successfully accomplished. The ball was flattened against my ribs; two of them were splintered, and pieces of them occasionally worked out through the wound during the ensuing eight months. Because of the fracture of my ribs and the wound in my back, I was obliged to lie on one hip, with the result that I suffered from severe bedsores, and for weeks was able to get sleep only by taking morphine.

In October of that year the surgeons decided that it would do to remove me to my home at Dobbs Ferry on the Hudson.

During the following winter I was confined to my bed at intervals by abscesses forming preliminary to their discharging pieces of bone or cloth, the last particles coming out the following March or April. The wound healed in June, though my body was bent and one leg contracted. Hence I was obliged to walk with a cane for nearly another year, although I was able to perform clerical work that summer.

Chapter 16

The Generals

General D. McM. Gregg was a West Point graduate and had seen service in the army before the war. He was dignified in manner and that winter I was more or less in awe of him, when in his presence. One day he sent for me and asked me if I knew of a certain special order from the War Department bearing on a certain subject. Replying, "I think it is number so and so," he said: "You should not think, sir, you should know. Go and find out." To a layman this might seem needlessly severe, but it was just the kind of training the young volunteer soldiers needed. Indeed, my after experience demonstrated that one could not have been under a more considerate and finer commander.

His coolness whenever we were in action and his thoughtfulness in looking out for his men, sparing them needless risks and taking precautions to protect them from surprises, secured for him the absolute confidence of every one in his command. He was averse to newspaper notoriety and I do not recall an instance when he seemed willing to give information to reporters. His idea was to confine what he had to tell to his official reports, and let the records testify to the character of his service. Indeed, on one occasion he remarked to me, "Meyer, I do not propose to have a picture reputation." As I am writing these lines he is still living, beloved by the survivors of those who served under him and respected by the people of Pennsylvania, the State in which he lives.

General Judson Kilpatrick, also a West Point graduate, was of slight build, wiry, apparently incapable of fatigue, and physically just the man for a cavalry leader. He was of a highly excitable and nervous temperament. Whenever we reached camp and everyone else seemed to think that men and horses should have a rest, Kilpatrick was writing letters and asking for authority from his superiors to start out on a reconnoissance or a raid, or to give him a chance to get into a fight. I was told that when at West Point he was noted for making speeches. With us he would frequently harangue the men, but his good-natured dash and personal magnetism made him popular.

He had capacity for rallying his soldiers and getting them into a charge. His usual method when meeting the enemy was to order a charge. Sometimes this was very successful, and at other times it was not so much so and very costly of men. It was because of this that he secured the nickname of "Kil-Cavalry." He was good-natured, approachable, and not inclined to be much of a disciplinarian.

He was not disposed to punish his men if they took a horse from citizens, which they occasionally did in 1862, unless they were caught at it.

One day when we were in camp near Falmouth a citizen called on him to complain that a horse of his had been stolen and to ask permission to go through our companies' streets in search of it. The man rode into camp and tied his horse to one of the stakes to which the general's tent was attached. Kilpatrick courteously invited him in, listened to his story, and gave him permission to go through camp looking for his horse. On emerging from the tent the man found that while he was inside someone had taken his saddle from the horse he rode in on. My recollection is that he recovered neither the saddle nor the horse he was in search of.

Kilpatrick was energetic, brave, and patriotic, and as a cavalry leader had a splendid record, and I understood that his services after he went to Sherman's army were much appreciated by that commander.

Among the fine officers with whom it was my privilege to serve and whose friendship has grown and still exists, were Colonel Henry C. Weir, adjutant-general of General D. McM. Gregg's cavalry division and his chief-of-staff, and General Walter C. Newberry, the lieutenant-colonel commanding the Twenty-fourth cavalry in June. It was the former who took me from the ranks and secured for me the position at General Gregg's headquarters, which brought me under the eye of the General and gave me opportunities that probably secured the promotion I ultimately obtained.

Weir was about twenty-one years of age in 1863, and with a most attractive personality. He had a wide acquaintance among officers of the army who had graduated from West Point, since his father was Professor Weir, the famous artist on duty there, some of whose paintings are in the rotunda of the Capitol at Washington. Weir was adjutant-general of General Bayard's brigade when the latter was killed at Fredericksburg, and then continued as such with General Gregg's division to the end of the war. He was intensely patriotic, high-toned in character, and one of the bravest men I ever knew.

Indeed, General Gregg once remarked to me after the war that Weir was so uniformly brave that he found it difficult to recall a particular instance in order that he might recommend him for a Medal of Honor. The Medal of Honor was, however, awarded to Weir later and no man better deserved it.

General Newberry, to whose kindness and consideration I am so greatly indebted, had been an officer in one of the New York State infantry regiments that went out for two years' service. On returning in 1863, he, with Colonel W. C. Raulston, raised the Twenty-fourth New York cavalry. These officers were both fine soldiers.

General Newberry was a man of sound judgment, exceedingly cool in battle and in emergencies, and a fine executive. He was most considerate of his men and quick to appreciate any man or officer who tried to do his duty. I doubt if any colonel of a regiment knew more of his men personally than did he. He kept a record in which he described the character of every officer's service, noting his impression of them both as men and officers. Since the war he has been a man of affairs, holding prominent positions, serving his city, State, and nation, yet with all his large interests he has kept himself informed of the whereabouts of many of the survivors of the Twenty-fourth cavalry, and I cannot imagine any regimental commander more beloved by his men than he.

During my short term of service with the Twenty-fourth cavalry, which was from about the latter part of February till the 17th of June, the last forty-five days of which covered the campaign from the Wilderness to Petersburg, my intercourse with General Newberry was mainly official, and it was not until I received a sympathetic letter[1] while in the hospital that I realized how good a friend I had in him. In later years this letter was followed by a report to the Secretary of War recommending that a Medal of Honor be awarded me, which was accordingly done.[2]

In October, the 24th New York cavalry was mounted and assigned to General Gregg's division, which in the spring of 1865 was commanded by General Crook. Except when commanding a brigade,

1. See Appendix B.
2. See Appendix A.

General Newberry commanded the regiment from June 18th, when Colonel Raulston was wounded, until a few days before the end of the war. He was wounded twice in the summer of 1864, but retained his command until March 31, 1865, at Dinwiddie Court House, where he was severely wounded, this preventing further active service. Lee's surrender occurred ten days later. He was brevetted brigadier-general for gallant and distinguished service at Dinwiddie Court House, March 31, 1865.

I count the friendship of Newberry and Weir, begun during the war and continuing up to the present time, one of the greatest privileges I have ever been able to enjoy.

Colonel William C. Raulston, who commanded the Twenty-fourth cavalry until he was given the command of a brigade, also treated me with great courtesy and consideration. It was he who suggested that I be selected to go to Washington for ammunition, and I assume he also recommended me for other special duties which I was given an opportunity to perform. He was an exceedingly gallant officer, was wounded on the day after I was, recovered and returned to duty, and was subsequently captured. In an unsuccessful attempt to break out of prison at Danville, in which he was a leader, he was shot by a guard and died a few days after.

Among the many gallant men with whom I at different times served, I remember especially Captain L. G. Estes, adjutant-general to General Kilpatrick, and afterwards Brevet Brigadier-General, and his aides, Captain, afterwards Brevet Brigadier-General, E. W. Whitaker and Captain Theodore F. Northrop. No cavalry officer had braver staff-officers than were these three men. Whitaker and Northrop repeatedly carried out successfully missions involving unusual hazards and requiring great daring.

Appendix A

Chicago, Ill.,
April 11, 1898.

Hon. Russell A. Alger,
Secy. of War,
Washington, D. C.

Dear Sir:

I believe there are still some Medals of Honour awaiting officers and men of the late War who by some special act of bravery or the saving of life or enhancing the safety of the Army have earned such a reward.

I desire to call your attention to the case of an officer of my own Regiment, the 24th N.Y. Cavalry, who has suffered greatly, and who has achieved most honorable position in the scientific world as a citizen since the War. I speak of Capt. and Brevet Major Henry C. Meyer, now Editor and Proprietor of a publication known as the *Engineering Record* of New York City. He has two sons who were raised in the same honorable manner and promise the very best of American citizenship to their country that their father has, and I should very much like to see the father's heroism and suffering rewarded as they deserve and as I believe the Government intended by these Medals of Honor.

Meyer as a boy, against his father's desire, enlisted in '62 in what was known as the "Harris Light" (2nd New York Cavalry). Being of good education and writing a fine hand, he was subsequently detailed as a clerk at Headquarters of General D. McM. Gregg of the 2nd Division of Cavalry. On the 9th of June, '63, at Brandy Station, noticing some men hard pressed, he rushed into the thickest of the fight and was wounded by a sabre across the shoulder. He made light of the wound at the time and induced Adj.-General Weir not to report his name as wounded on account of needless alarm to his mother.

Within the last few years, however, both General Gregg and Colonel Weir reported this circumstance to the War Department, which you will find on file under date of November 19th, '91, addressed to the Adj.-General of the Army and certified by those officers.

Later, in an engagement at Buckland Mills, where General Kilpatrick's Division met with a reverse, General Davies's Brigade was imperilled by reason of the fact that General Custer's Brigade had been driven to the north side of Broad Run, and the enemy had gotten in between General Custer and his command, which was hard pressed some two miles near Warrenton.

General Kilpatrick expressed his desire that somebody get to Davies that he might be made aware of the situation. Without waiting for further orders Meyer rode up the river and crossed the stream above the enemy and made his way around their flank and in their rear to Davies, who was thus enabled, without serious loss, to escape across the country to Haymarket. Meyer was recommended by Generals Gregg and Kilpatrick for a commission, and early in '64 was assigned to the 24th New York Cavalry, then just ready for the field. Coming to us with a 2nd Lieut.'s commission and being familiar with cavalry tactics he was a great addition to our effectiveness.

From the Wilderness through that entire campaign the 24th N. Y. fought dismounted, and Lt. Meyer was most efficient from the fact of knowing the country so well, and was frequently detailed to guide troops to positions, especially about Spottsylvania.

The Regiment being armed with special Star Carbines used a special cartridge unobtainable except by special requisition, and the Regiment being in constant service at the front, the ammunition was likely to be exhausted. Gen. Burnside was requested to send an officer to Washington for these cartridges, and he by special letter detailed Lt. Meyer, who showed great efficiency in bringing the ammunition to the front, seizing a wagon of Gen. Potter's (another Division) to save time and distributing the cartridges in blankets along the line of battle when the supply was nearly exhausted.

On the 8th of June Meyer was commissioned Captain, and on June 17th, in that terrible assault upon the line before Petersburg, where he lost one third of his Company, he was fearfully wounded very near the position where Gen. Morton, the Engineer Officer of the Corps, was killed. He had escaped wounds through the most serious part of the charge, when later he discovered an officer, Lt. Randall, very badly wounded, Randall having been shot in five places and lying with his face buried in the dirt between our lines; Meyer turned back, going fifty to seventy-five yards out of his way, and in plain sight of the enemy, turned Lt. Randall over, brushed the sand and blood from his mouth so that he could breathe, thus saving his life, when he himself received a most dangerous wound.

I was in sight of him, and he, after crawling in, was helped over the works just in advance of me by two men, and as soon as I reached him I detailed men to carry him back. For many months he lay in the Hospital and was not able to be removed to his home until the following October, and was a great sufferer for eleven months.

I should claim that this act alone of saving the life of a brother officer, being an act beyond his regular duty, entitled him to a Medal of Honour. His service and his honourable character as a civilian and the high position he today holds in the scientific world seem to point him out as a proper person to receive such high and distinguishing honour from the Government. I earnestly recommend that the Medal of Honour be conferred upon Captain and Brevet Major Henry C. Meyer of New York City.

With continued high regard,

 I remain,

  Respectfully,

   Walter C. Newberry,

    Late Col. 24th N.Y. Vet. Cavl.

   Brevet Brig. Genl.

E. L.
Subject: Medal of Honour.

WAR DEPARTMENT,
WASHINGTON.

File No. R. & P. 517,138.

March 14, 1899.

Captain Henry C. Meyer,
The Engineering Record,
277 Pearl Street,
New York City.

Sir:

I have the honour to advise you that, by direction of the President and under the provisions of the Act of Congress approved March 3, 1863, a Congressional Medal of Honour has this day been awarded to you for distinguished gallantry in action near Petersburg, Virginia, June 17, 1864, the following being a statement of the particular service rendered on that occasion:

> During an assault upon the enemy's works, this officer rendered heroic assistance to a helpless brother officer in the face of a heavy fire, thereby saving his life, and in the performance of this gallant act sustained a severe wound.

The Medal will be forwarded to you, by registered mail, as soon as it shall have been properly engraved.

Very respectfully,

G. D. Meikeljohn,
Assistant Secretary of War.

EXTRACT FROM GENERAL NEWBERRY'S RECORDS

Chicago, April 11, 1898.

Henry C. Meyer, Jr.,
New York City.

My Dear Sir:

Soon after the close of the War of the Rebellion, finding myself in possession of the Descriptive List Roster of my Regiment— the 24th N. Y. Veteran Cavalry,—and appreciating the effect of time upon my memory and judgment, resolved to go over the list of officers and make record of my unbiased conclusion as to their ability and character.

I have had frequent occasion to consult that record since, and knowing how much you would appreciate this recorded opinion of your Father's character and service I will quote my endorsement as therein written thirty-three years ago.

Henry C. Meyer, 2nd Lt, Jan. 26, 1864. Promoted to Capt. June 8, 1864.

Assigned to Co. D. Wounded June 17, 1864.

Discharged Sp. Order War Dept. Oct. 13, 1864; Disability.

This officer was among the finest officers I have ever met. Cool, cautious, and brave as a soldier, he was generous, true, and sincere as a friend. He was fearfully wounded and was discharged in consequence.

W. C. Newberry,
Col.

May you deserve such commendation after as many years of experience.

Sincerely yours,
Walter C. Newberry.

Appendix B

[The following letters and copies of special orders are here reproduced as having some bearing on my promotions, and to indicate the opinions of those with whom I actively served in the Civil War of 1861-1865.—H. C. M.]

FIRST PROMOTION

Head Quarters Cavalry Division.
Left Grand Division.
Dec. 29th, 1862.

Special Order
No. 7.

Private Henry C. Meyer, of C Company, 2nd New York Cavalry, is hereby detailed as Clerk in the Adjt. Genl's office at these Head Quarters and will report immediately.

By command of Brig. Genl. Gregg.

H. C. Weir,
Capt. and A. A. G.

(Official Copy.)
H. C. Weir,
Capt. and A. A. G.

RECOMMENDATIONS FOR COMMISSION

Head Quarters 2nd Div. Cav.,
Ass't Adj't Genl's Office,
Sept. 5th, 1863.

Hon. Geo. T. Cobb, M. C.

Sir:

It gives me pleasure to recommend Private Henry C. Meyer, 2nd N. York Cav., for a commission. He has been a faithful soldier and excellent clerk, and is eminently qualified mentally and morally for a commission, especially as an adjutant of a Regiment.

I am very respectfully.

Your obedient servant,

H. C. Weir

A. A. G.

Head Qrs., 2nd Div. Cav. Corps,

Sept. 6th, 1863.

The within recommendation of Capt. H. C. Weir, A. A. G., of this Division, is fully concurred in. I have known Private Meyer, 2nd N.Y. Cavalry, for nearly two years and can attest his faithfulness as a soldier, his moral, mental, and physical qualifications for the position of Commissioned Officer.

D. McM. Gregg,

Brig. Gen. Vols.,

Com'g, 2nd Div.,

Cavalry Corps.

Headquarters 2nd Division Cavalry Corps,

September 9th, 1863.

Lieut. E. B. Parsons,

A. A. A. G. Cavalry Corps.

Lieut.:

I have the honour to request the suspension of the order from the Major General Commanding directing me to return Private H. C. Meyer, 2nd New York Cavalry, to his Regiment. Private Meyer has been serving for a year as clerk at the Hdqrs. of the 2nd Division, the former 3rd Division, and Bayard's Brigade. He is well instructed in his duties, and is familiar with all the records of the Adjutant-General's office of this Division. Capt. H. C. Weir, A. A. G., of this Division, is now absent sick, and at this time the services of Private Meyer are invaluable. I respectfully request, therefore, that I may for the present be permitted to retain Private Meyer.

Private W. H. Bubier, 2nd N. Y. Cavalry, was taken prisoner at the battle of Brandy Station, and has not returned to these Headquarters.

I am, very respectfully,

Your obedient servant,

D. McM. Gregg,
Brig.-Gen'l Vols.,
Comdg 2nd Divsn., C. C.

(Official copy)
H. C. Weir,
Capt. A. A. G.

Head Quarters 3rd Division,
Cavalry Corps,
Octr. 5th, 1863.

Special Order
No. 38.

Private Henry C. Meyer, Co. C, 2nd N. York Cavalry, is hereby detailed on special duty as Clerk in the Adjt. Genl's Office at these Head Quarters, and will report for duty without delay. By command of Brig.-Genl. Kilpatrick.

L. G. Estes,
A. A. Genl.

(Official)
L. G. Estes,
A. A. G.

RECOMMENDATIONS FOR PROMOTION TO A COMMISSIONED OFFICER

Head Quarters, 3rd Division, C. C.
December 31st, 1863.

Hon. Geo. T. Cobb:

I understand that you are about to make an effort to secure a Lieutenancy in one of the regular Cav. Regiments for Henry C. Meyer, now a private in Harris Light Cavalry. I hope you will be successful; he fully merits and will fill with honor the position to which he aspires. He was for a long time a clerk at General Gregg's head quarters, and after I was given a division transferred to my headquarters. He is energetic, well educated, and a gentleman, and possessing as he does a thorough knowledge of all papers, accounts, and reports which pertain to a regiment, brigade, or division, acquired by one or two years' service in the field, he is better qualified to discharge the duties of a subordinate officer than many of our West Point graduates on leaving the Academy. If you think this letter will aid in your efforts you are at liberty to use it.

Very Respectfully,

Your Obedient Servant,

J. Kilpatrick,

Brig. Genl.Vols.

LETTER ACCOMPANYING MY COMMISSION WHILE IN SEMINARY HOSPITAL

Head Quarters 24th N.Y. Cavalry,
Near Petersburg, Va., July 22, '64.

My Dear Capt:

Your commission has arrived and I have forwarded it to your address at the Metropolitan Hotel, Washington. D. C, thinking it would be more safe than at the Hospital, for we're not certain where you are now. I congratulate you on the promotion and am happy to acknowledge that you deserve it and much more than a bleeding, suffering country like ours can ever give. These honours but illy pay a man for the suffering endured, where horrible wounds like yours are the penalty of bravery. Yet the consciousness of having done one's duty is much reward.

We all look for your return with much interest. Lt. Raulston is today mustered to your Company. I enclose a morning report of your Co.

With many wishes for your health, I am,

Yours,

Newberry,

Lt-Col. Comdg.

Capt. Henry C. Meyer.

FINAL DISCHARGE ON ACCOUNT OF DISABILITY FROM WOUNDS

War Department,
Adjt. Genl's Office, Washington, D. C.
October 13th, 1864.

Special Order
No. 345.

(Extract.)

51. The following named officers are hereby honourably discharged the Service of the United States on account of physical disability from wounds received in action, with condition that

they shall receive no final payments until they have satisfied the Pay Department that they are not indebted to the Government.

2nd Lt. H. C. Meyer, 24th N.Y. Cav'y.[1]

By Order of the Secretary of War.

E. A. Townsend,

A. A. Gen'l.

Hd. Qrs. 2nd Cav. Division,

Oct. 23rd, '64.

(Official.)

A. H. Bibber,

A. A. A. Gen'l.

Hd. Qrs. 24th N.Y. Cavly.,

Feb. 20th, 1865.

C. P. Williams,

(Official Copy.)   Lt. and Act. Adjt.

[THE FOLLOWING LETTER WAS NEVER PRESENTED.]

Navy Yard, New York,

Decr. 23rd, 1863.

My Dear Mr. Potts:

The bearer of this is Henry C. Meyer, my young friend who has gallantly served in the field with Generals Kilpatrick and Gregg.

He is to my knowledge a gentleman by education and association, and in every way calculated to fill the place of a First Lieutenant.

I have given a letter to the Adjut-General, and if you can speak a good word for him you will do me a great kindness.

All his attributes are those of a gentleman.

Your friend,

H. Paulding.

John Potts, Esq.,

Chief Clerk, War Department.

---

1. I was discharged as 2nd Lieutenant because no opportunity occurred to permit my being mustered in as Captain before I was wounded. Congress, however, recognized all such cases, and subsequent legislation gave all officers the rank they were eligible to—mine being Captain. Subsequently I received a commission as Brevet Major, stated to be for "gallant and meritorious services."—H. C. M.

Navy Yard, New York,
Dec. 23rd, 1863.

Sir: I take leave, most respectfully, to commend to your Excellency's consideration my young friend, Henry C. Meyer, a private in Second N.Y. Light Cavalry. He is intelligent, of a highly interesting and unexceptionable character, well educated, and in all his attributes of a gentleman well calculated to fill the place of an officer.

He has been serving in the field with Generals Kilpatrick and Gregg for eighteen months, and his commanding officers testify to his gallantry and his manly bearing.

In speaking thus highly of Mr. Meyer I do so from personal knowledge, having known him from a child.

I trust your Excellency may be able to advance this young gentleman to a position worthy of his merit, feeling assured it will be for the interest of the public service.

With high respect, your Excellency's most obedient servant,

H. Paulding,
Rear Admiral.

His Excellency,
 Horatio Seymour,
  Governor of the State of New York.

Navy Yard, New York,
December 23rd, 1863.

My Dear General:

My young friend, Henry C. Meyer, of the 2nd N. York Light Cavalry, has been serving in the field with Generals Kilpatrick and Gregg for eighteen months as a private, and his gallantry and manly bearing are well attested.

I have known him from childhood as estimable and charming in all his attributes as a gentleman.

He is well educated, high-toned in character, and in every way a young gentleman of great merit.

He entered the service from the love of a soldier's life and motives of patriotism.

He has won advancement by his service in the field and will make an excellent officer.

If you can give him a helping hand, I am sure you will. I have no acquaintance with the Sec. of War or General-in-Chief, and therefore commend the young gentleman to you as one of our fraternity when the Rebellion commenced.

I have the honour to be, with high respect and esteem, your friend and most obedient servant

H. Paulding,
Rear Admiral.

To Genl. E. D. Townsend,
    Adjt. Genl., U. S. Army,
        Washington.

(True copy.)

War Department,
Adjutant-General's Office,
Washington, February 10th, 1864.

Special Order
  No. 66

(*Extract.*)

14. At the request of the Governor of New York, Private Henry C. Meyer, 2nd New York Cavalry, is hereby honourably discharged the Service of the United States to enable him to accept an appointment in another Regiment.

By order of the Secretary of War,
E. D. Townsend,
Asst. Adjutant Gen.

Head Quarters Cavalry Corps,
    Feb. 12th, 1864.
(Official.)
    E. B. Parsons,

Capt. and A. A. A. G.

Head Quarters 3rd Div. C. C,
Feb. 12th, 1864.

(Official.)   L. G. Estes,

Capt. and A. A. G.

ADMIRAL PAULDING TO GENERAL KILPATRICK.

Navy Yard, New York,
February 16th, 1864.

My Dear General:

Without a personal acquaintance, I respect and honour you for gallant service in the field.

You have had my young friend Henry Meyer with you and have learned to esteem him. I have known him from a boy, as an interesting youth, and as a gentleman by education and association, and know that when he entered the Army as a private he was honoured and beloved, and from zeal and love of country he left a comfortable home and lucrative place.

I am very fond of him for his personal merit and have confidence in commending him to you in every way in which he can serve you in our sacred cause.

He is now a 2nd Lieut. in a New York Regt. and will doubtless be able soon to fill a more prominent place.

For the favour you have shown him, and for your gallant and distinguished services to the country, I entertain the highest respect for you and thank and honour you and beg to subscribe myself your friend and most obedient servant.

H. Paulding,

Rear Admiral and Comdt.

To Genl. J. Kilpatrick,
    Army of the Potomac.

EXPLANATION OF NON-MUSTER AS CAPTAIN.

I hereby certify that Henry C. Meyer, late 2nd Lieutenant 24th N.Y. Cavalry, was severely wounded in action on the 17th day of June before Petersburg, Va., 1864; that there was a Commission from the Governor of New York making said Meyer a Captain in said Regiment, and that owing to an irregularity in the mails said Commission did not arrive at the Head Quarters of the command until about the 20th inst.; and further, that said Meyer was acting in the capacity of Captain by authority of the Col. commanding, and that he was absent and prevented from being mustered by no fault of his; that said Meyer was a gallant and meritorious officer and deserving said promotion.

W. C. Newberry,

Late Col. 24th N.Y. Cavalry.

Bvt. Brig. Gen.

Sworn subscribed to before me
this 19th day of June, 1866, at
this city of Petersburg, Va.
Chas. Stringfellen,
[Seal]   Notary Public.

West Seneca Centre, N.Y.

October 14th, 1868.

Capt. H. C. Meyer,

New York City.

Dear Sir: A few days back I was in Buffalo and stopped at Mr.
Flach's store; I learned that you got married. Permit me, dear sir,
to give you my best and sincere congratulation.

I always must and will respect you for your honesty, bravery,
and your good moralic advices, which you used to give your
subordinate. When others did their duty, you used to do three
times more than you was obliged to do.

I would ask you for your likeness.

Your most obedient servant,

Fred. Gundlach.

New York, November 19, 1891.

To the Adjutant-General of the Army,

Washington, D. C.

Dear Sir: At the solicitation of friends I desire to place on record
the fact, not heretofore officially reported, that I received a
wound from a sabre at the battle of Brandy Station on the 9th
of June, 1863.

I was then a private in the 2nd N.Y. Cavalry, detailed as clerk in
the Adjutant-General's Department of the 2nd Division Cavalry Corps, Army of the Potomac.

That this circumstance was not reported at the time was due to
the fact that I personally made out the list of casualties occurring in the Division on the evening following the battle. My
wound was not a severe one, though painful.

When it was suggested that I include my name, I declined to do
so on the ground that its publication in the papers would needlessly alarm my parents, and consequently withheld it.

I was subsequently severely wounded at Petersburg and mustered out in consequence, which is a matter of record.

In making this request to have this circumstance go on record, I disclaim any permanent injury or any desire or intention of claiming any pension because of that wound.

This statement is corroborated herewith by General D. McM. Gregg, commanding the Division, and H. C. Weir, Capt. and Asst. Adjutant-General at the time.

Respectfully,

Henry C. Meyer.

Late Capt. and Bvt. Major,

24th New York Cavalry.

The above was endorsed as follows:

The foregoing statement is correct and worthy of record, and I heartily recommend the same.

Very respectfully, your obedient servant,

Henry C. Weir,

Late Bv't Lt. Col. and Major,

Ass't Adjt. Gen'l, U. S. Vols.,

2nd Division, Cavalry Corps,

A. O. Potomac.

Brooklyn, L. I., Nov. 25, '91.

Reading, Pa., Dec. 5th, 1891.

I fully concur in the recommendation of Colonel Weir, as I readily recall the fact mentioned within.

D. Mc.M. Gregg,

Late Brig. and Bv't Maj. Gen'l Vols.,

Com'd'g 2nd Cav. Division, A. P.

LEONAUR

ALSO FROM LEONAUR
AVAILABLE IN SOFTCOVER OR HARDCOVER WITH DUST JACKET

THE 2ND MAORI WAR: 1860-1861 *by Robert Carey*—The Second Maori War, or First Taranaki War, one more bloody instalment of the conflicts between European settlers and the indigenous Maori people.

A JOURNAL OF THE SECOND SIKH WAR *by Daniel A. Sandford*—The Experiences of an Ensign of the 2nd Bengal European Regiment During the Campaign in the Punjab, India, 1848-49.

THE LIGHT INFANTRY OFFICER *by John H. Cooke*—The Experiences of an Officer of the 43rd Light Infantry in America During the War of 1812.

BUSHVELDT CARBINEERS *by George Witton*—The War Against the Boers in South Africa and the 'Breaker' Morant Incident.

LAKE'S CAMPAIGNS IN INDIA *by Hugh Pearse*—The Second Anglo Maratha War, 1803-1807.

BRITAIN IN AFGHANISTAN 1: THE FIRST AFGHAN WAR 1839-42 *by Archibald Forbes*—From invasion to destruction-a British military disaster.

BRITAIN IN AFGHANISTAN 2: THE SECOND AFGHAN WAR 1878-80 *by Archibald Forbes*—This is the history of the Second Afghan War-another episode of British military history typified by savagery, massacre, siege and battles.

UP AMONG THE PANDIES *by Vivian Dering Majendie*—Experiences of a British Officer on Campaign During the Indian Mutiny, 1857-1858.

MUTINY: 1857 *by James Humphries*—Authentic Voices from the Indian Mutiny-First Hand Accounts of Battles, Sieges and Personal Hardships.

BLOW THE BUGLE, DRAW THE SWORD *by W. H. G. Kingston*—The Wars, Campaigns, Regiments and Soldiers of the British & Indian Armies During the Victorian Era, 1839-1898.

WAR BEYOND THE DRAGON PAGODA *by Major J. J. Snodgrass*—A Personal Narrative of the First Anglo-Burmese War 1824 - 1826.

THE HERO OF ALIWAL *by James Humphries*—The Campaigns of Sir Harry Smith in India, 1843-1846, During the Gwalior War & the First Sikh War.

ALL FOR A SHILLING A DAY *by Donald F. Featherstone*—The story of H.M. 16th, the Queen's Lancers During the first Sikh War 1845-1846.

LEONAUR

ALSO FROM LEONAUR
AVAILABLE IN SOFTCOVER OR HARDCOVER WITH DUST JACKET

AT THEM WITH THE BAYONET *by Donald F. Featherstone*—The first Anglo-Sikh War 1845-1846.

STEPHEN CRANE'S BATTLES *by Stephen Crane*—Nine Decisive Battles Recounted by the Author of 'The Red Badge of Courage'.

THE GURKHA WAR *by H. T. Prinsep*—The Anglo-Nepalese Conflict in North East India 1814-1816.

FIRE & BLOOD *by G. R. Gleig*—The burning of Washington & the battle of New Orleans, 1814, through the eyes of a young British soldier.

SOUND ADVANCE! *by Joseph Anderson*—Experiences of an officer of HM 50th regiment in Australia, Burma & the Gwalior war.

THE CAMPAIGN OF THE INDUS *by Thomas Holdsworth*—Experiences of a British Officer of the 2nd (Queen's Royal) Regiment in the Campaign to Place Shah Shuja on the Throne of Afghanistan 1838 - 1840.

WITH THE MADRAS EUROPEAN REGIMENT IN BURMA *by John Butler*—The Experiences of an Officer of the Honourable East India Company's Army During the First Anglo-Burmese War 1824 - 1826.

IN ZULULAND WITH THE BRITISH ARMY *by Charles L. Norris-Newman*—The Anglo-Zulu war of 1879 through the first-hand experiences of a special correspondent.

BESIEGED IN LUCKNOW *by Martin Richard Gubbins*—The first Anglo-Sikh War 1845-1846.

A TIGER ON HORSEBACK *by L. March Phillips*—The Experiences of a Trooper & Officer of Rimington's Guides - The Tigers during the Anglo-Boer war 1899 - 1902.

SEPOYS, SIEGE & STORM *by Charles John Griffiths*—The Experiences of a young officer of H.M.'s 61st Regiment at Ferozepore, Delhi ridge and at the fall of Delhi during the Indian mutiny 1857.

CAMPAIGNING IN ZULULAND *by W. E. Montague*—Experiences on campaign during the Zulu war of 1879 with the 94th Regiment.

THE STORY OF THE GUIDES *by G.J. Younghusband*—The Exploits of the Soldiers of the famous Indian Army Regiment from the northwest frontier 1847 - 1900.

LEONAUR

ALSO FROM LEONAUR
AVAILABLE IN SOFTCOVER OR HARDCOVER WITH DUST JACKET

OFFICERS & GENTLEMEN *by Peter Hawker & William Graham*—Two Accounts of British Officers During the Peninsula War: Officer of Light Dragoons by Peter Hawker & Campaign in Portugal and Spain by William Graham .

THE WALCHEREN EXPEDITION *by Anonymous*—The Experiences of a British Officer of the 81st Regt. During the Campaign in the Low Countries of 1809.

LADIES OF WATERLOO *by Charlotte A. Eaton, Magdalene de Lancey & Juana Smith*—The Experiences of Three Women During the Campaign of 1815: Waterloo Days by Charlotte A. Eaton, A Week at Waterloo by Magdalene de Lancey & Juana's Story by Juana Smith.

JOURNAL OF AN OFFICER IN THE KING'S GERMAN LEGION *by John Frederick Hering*—Recollections of Campaigning During the Napoleonic Wars.

JOURNAL OF AN ARMY SURGEON IN THE PENINSULAR WAR *by Charles Boutflower*—The Recollections of a British Army Medical Man on Campaign During the Napoleonic Wars.

ON CAMPAIGN WITH MOORE AND WELLINGTON *by Anthony Hamilton*—The Experiences of a Soldier of the 43rd Regiment During the Peninsular War.

THE ROAD TO AUSTERLITZ *by R. G. Burton*—Napoleon's Campaign of 1805.

SOLDIERS OF NAPOLEON *by A. J. Doisy De Villargennes & Arthur Chuquet*—The Experiences of the Men of the French First Empire: Under the Eagles by A. J. Doisy De Villargennes & Voices of 1812 by Arthur Chuquet .

INVASION OF FRANCE, 1814 *by F. W. O. Maycock*—The Final Battles of the Napoleonic First Empire.

LEIPZIG—A CONFLICT OF TITANS *by Frederic Shoberl*—A Personal Experience of the 'Battle of the Nations' During the Napoleonic Wars, October 14th-19th, 1813.

SLASHERS *by Charles Cadell*—The Campaigns of the 28th Regiment of Foot During the Napoleonic Wars by a Serving Officer.

BATTLE IMPERIAL *by Charles William Vane*—The Campaigns in Germany & France for the Defeat of Napoleon 1813-1814.

SWIFT & BOLD *by Gibbes Rigaud*—The 60th Rifles During the Peninsula War.

LEONAUR

ALSO FROM LEONAUR
AVAILABLE IN SOFTCOVER OR HARDCOVER WITH DUST JACKET

OMPTEDA OF THE KING'S GERMAN LEGION *by Christian von Ompteda*—A Hanoverian Officer on Campaign Against Napoleon.

LIEUTENANT SIMMONS OF THE 95TH (RIFLES) *by George Simmons*—Recollections of the Peninsula, South of France & Waterloo Campaigns of the Napoleonic Wars.

A HORSEMAN FOR THE EMPEROR *by Jean Baptiste Gazzola*—A Cavalryman of Napoleon's Army on Campaign Throughout the Napoleonic Wars.

SERGEANT LAWRENCE *by William Lawrence*—With the 40th Regt. of Foot in South America, the Peninsular War & at Waterloo.

CAMPAIGNS WITH THE FIELD TRAIN *by Richard D. Henegan*—Experiences of a British Officer During the Peninsula and Waterloo Campaigns of the Napoleonic Wars.

CAVALRY SURGEON *by S. D. Broughton*—On Campaign Against Napoleon in the Peninsula & South of France During the Napoleonic Wars 1812-1814.

MEN OF THE RIFLES *by Thomas Knight, Henry Curling & Jonathan Leach*—The Reminiscences of Thomas Knight of the 95th (Rifles) by Thomas Knight, Henry Curling's Anecdotes by Henry Curling & The Field Services of the Rifle Brigade from its Formation to Waterloo by Jonathan Leach.

THE ULM CAMPAIGN 1805 *by F. N. Maude*—Napoleon and the Defeat of the Austrian Army During the 'War of the Third Coalition'.

SOLDIERING WITH THE 'DIVISION' *by Thomas Garrety*—The Military Experiences of an Infantryman of the 43rd Regiment During the Napoleonic Wars.

SERGEANT MORRIS OF THE 73RD FOOT *by Thomas Morris*—The Experiences of a British Infantryman During the Napoleonic Wars-Including Campaigns in Germany and at Waterloo.

A VOICE FROM WATERLOO *by Edward Cotton*—The Personal Experiences of a British Cavalryman Who Became a Battlefield Guide and Authority on the Campaign of 1815.

NAPOLEON AND HIS MARSHALS *by J. T. Headley*—The Men of the First Empire.

LEONAUR

ALSO FROM LEONAUR

AVAILABLE IN SOFTCOVER OR HARDCOVER WITH DUST JACKET

THE LIFE OF THE REAL BRIGADIER GERARD VOLUME 1—THE YOUNG HUSSAR 1782-1807 *by Jean-Baptiste De Marbot*—A French Cavalryman Of the Napoleonic Wars at Marengo, Austerlitz, Jena, Eylau & Friedland.

THE LIFE OF THE REAL BRIGADIER GERARD VOLUME 2—IMPERIAL AIDE-DE-CAMP 1807-1811 *by Jean-Baptiste De Marbot*—A French Cavalryman of the Napoleonic Wars at Saragossa, Landshut, Eckmuhl, Ratisbon, Aspern-Essling, Wagram, Busaco & Torres Vedras.

THE LIFE OF THE REAL BRIGADIER GERARD VOLUME 3—COLONEL OF CHASSEURS 1811-1815 *by Jean-Baptiste De Marbot*—A French Cavalryman in the retreat from Moscow, Lutzen, Bautzen, Katzbach, Leipzig, Hanau & Waterloo.

THE INDIAN WAR OF 1864 *by Eugene Ware*—The Experiences of a Young Officer of the 7th Iowa Cavalry on the Western Frontier During the Civil War.

THE MARCH OF DESTINY *by Charles E. Young & V. Devinny*—Dangers of the Trail in 1865 by Charles E. Young & The Story of a Pioneer by V. Devinny, two Accounts of Early Emigrants to Colorado.

CROSSING THE PLAINS *by William Audley Maxwell*—A First Hand Narrative of the Early Pioneer Trail to California in 1857.

CHIEF OF SCOUTS *by William F. Drannan*—A Pilot to Emigrant and Government Trains, Across the Plains of the Western Frontier.

THIRTY-ONE YEARS ON THE PLAINS AND IN THE MOUNTAINS *by William F. Drannan*—William Drannan was born to be a pioneer, hunter, trapper and wagon train guide during the momentous days of the Great American West.

THE INDIAN WARS VOLUNTEER *by William Thompson*—Recollections of the Conflict Against the Snakes, Shoshone, Bannocks, Modocs and Other Native Tribes of the American North West.

THE 4TH TENNESSEE CAVALRY *by George B. Guild*—The Services of Smith's Regiment of Confederate Cavalry by One of its Officers.

COLONEL WORTHINGTON'S SHILOH *by T. Worthington*—The Tennessee Campaign, 1862, by an Officer of the Ohio Volunteers.

FOUR YEARS IN THE SADDLE *by W. L. Curry*—The History of the First Regiment Ohio Volunteer Cavalry in the American Civil War.

LEONAUR

ALSO FROM LEONAUR
AVAILABLE IN SOFTCOVER OR HARDCOVER WITH DUST JACKET

THE RELUCTANT REBEL by *William G. Stevenson*—A young Kentuckian's experiences in the Confederate Infantry & Cavalry during the American Civil War..

BOOTS AND SADDLES by *Elizabeth B. Custer*—The experiences of General Custer's Wife on the Western Plains.

FANNIE BEERS' CIVIL WAR by *Fannie A. Beers*—A Confederate Lady's Experiences of Nursing During the Campaigns & Battles of the American Civil War.

LADY SALE'S AFGHANISTAN by *Florentia Sale*—An Indomitable Victorian Lady's Account of the Retreat from Kabul During the First Afghan War.

THE TWO WARS OF MRS DUBERLY by *Frances Isabella Duberly*—An Intrepid Victorian Lady's Experience of the Crimea and Indian Mutiny.

THE REBELLIOUS DUCHESS by *Paul F. S. Dermoncourt*—The Adventures of the Duchess of Berri and Her Attempt to Overthrow French Monarchy.

LADIES OF WATERLOO by *Charlotte A. Eaton, Magdalene de Lancey & Juana Smith*—The Experiences of Three Women During the Campaign of 1815: Waterloo Days by Charlotte A. Eaton, A Week at Waterloo by Magdalene de Lancey & Juana's Story by Juana Smith.

TWO YEARS BEFORE THE MAST by *Richard Henry Dana. Jr.*—The account of one young man's experiences serving on board a sailing brig—the Penelope—bound for California, between the years 1834-36.

A SAILOR OF KING GEORGE by *Frederick Hoffman*—From Midshipman to Captain—Recollections of War at Sea in the Napoleonic Age 1793-1815.

LORDS OF THE SEA by *A. T. Mahan*—Great Captains of the Royal Navy During the Age of Sail.

COGGESHALL'S VOYAGES: VOLUME 1 by *George Coggeshall*—The Recollections of an American Schooner Captain.

COGGESHALL'S VOYAGES: VOLUME 2 by *George Coggeshall*—The Recollections of an American Schooner Captain.

TWILIGHT OF EMPIRE by *Sir Thomas Ussher & Sir George Cockburn*—Two accounts of Napoleon's Journeys in Exile to Elba and St. Helena: Narrative of Events by Sir Thomas Ussher & Napoleon's Last Voyage: Extract of a diary by Sir George Cockburn.

LEONAUR

ALSO FROM LEONAUR
AVAILABLE IN SOFTCOVER OR HARDCOVER WITH DUST JACKET

IRON TIMES WITH THE GUARDS *by An O. E. (G. P. A. Fildes)*—The Experiences of an Officer of the Coldstream Guards on the Western Front During the First World War.

THE GREAT WAR IN THE MIDDLE EAST: 1 *by W. T. Massey*—The Desert Campaigns & How Jerusalem Was Won---two classic accounts in one volume.

THE GREAT WAR IN THE MIDDLE EAST: 2 *by W. T. Massey*—Allenby's Final Triumph.

SMITH-DORRIEN *by Horace Smith-Dorrien*—Isandlwhana to the Great War.

1914 *by Sir John French*—The Early Campaigns of the Great War by the British Commander.

GRENADIER *by E. R. M. Fryer*—The Recollections of an Officer of the Grenadier Guards throughout the Great War on the Western Front.

BATTLE, CAPTURE & ESCAPE *by George Pearson*—The Experiences of a Canadian Light Infantryman During the Great War.

DIGGERS AT WAR *by R. Hugh Knyvett & G. P. Cuttriss*—"Over There" With the Australians by R. Hugh Knyvett and Over the Top With the Third Australian Division by G. P. Cuttriss. Accounts of Australians During the Great War in the Middle East, at Gallipoli and on the Western Front.

HEAVY FIGHTING BEFORE US *by George Brenton Laurie*—The Letters of an Officer of the Royal Irish Rifles on the Western Front During the Great War.

THE CAMELIERS *by Oliver Hogue*—A Classic Account of the Australians of the Imperial Camel Corps During the First World War in the Middle East.

RED DUST *by Donald Black*—A Classic Account of Australian Light Horsemen in Palestine During the First World War.

THE LEAN, BROWN MEN *by Angus Buchanan*—Experiences in East Africa During the Great War with the 25th Royal Fusiliers—the Legion of Frontiersmen.

THE NIGERIAN REGIMENT IN EAST AFRICA *by W. D. Downes*—On Campaign During the Great War 1916-1918.

THE 'DIE-HARDS' IN SIBERIA *by John Ward*—With the Middlesex Regiment Against the Bolsheviks 1918-19.

www.ingramcontent.com/pod-product-compliance
Lightning Source LLC
Chambersburg PA
CBHW031859090426
42741CB00005B/568